THE COMPLETE MUSICIAN

THE COMPLETE MUSICIAN

STUDENT WORKBOOK, VOLUME II

An Integrated Approach to Tonal
Theory, Analysis, and Listening

Steven G. Laitz
The Eastman School of Music

New York   Oxford
OXFORD UNIVERSITY PRESS
2003

Oxford University Press

Oxford   New York
Auckland   Bangkok   Buenos Aires   Cape Town   Chennai
Dar es Salaam   Delhi   Hong Kong   Istanbul   Karachi   Kolkata
Kuala Lumpur   Madrid   Melbourne   Mexico City   Mumbai
Nairobi   São Paulo   Shanghai   Taipei   Tokyo   Toronto

Published by Oxford University Press, Inc.
198 Madison Avenue, New York, New York 10016
http://www.oup-usa.org

Oxford is a registered trademark of Oxford University Press

ISBN 0-19-51606-06

Printing number: 9 8 7 6 5 4 3 2 1

Printed in the United States of America
on acid-free paper

CONTENTS

CHAPTER 20

Sequences within Larger Musical Contexts and Sequences with Seventh Chords

EXERCISE 20.1 Analysis of Sequential Progressions and Parallel $^6_3$ Passages

Bracket and label sequences, sequential progressions, and parallel $^6_3$ chord streams. Label suspensions and determine whether the $^6_3$ chords function transitionally or prolongationally.

A.   Handel, *Gigue,* Suite XVI in G minor, HWV 263
Consider this example to be in D minor. Make a 1:1 contrapuntal reduction of the excerpt. What long-range contrapuntal event takes place between the downbeats of m. 10 and m. 12?

d:

B.   Handel, "But Who May Abide the Day of His Coming?" *Messiah,* HWV 56
What contrapuntal technique is used at the beginning of this excerpt? Compare this example with the previous one.

C.   Schubert, German Dance No. 1, *German Dances and Ecossaises*, D. 643

D.   Corelli, *Corrente*, Concerto Grosso in C major, op. 6, no. 10

5   6   5   6   5   6   6   5   6   7   6   7   6   7   6   7   6   7   6

EXERCISE 20.2   Figured Bass

Realize the figured bass below, labeling all sequences. Analyze with two levels.
Sequence choices are as follows:

1.   D2 (D5/A4): $\frac{5}{3}$s, $\frac{6}{3}$s, sevenths (alternating or interlocking)
2.   A2 (A5/D4)
3.   D3 (D4/A2): $\frac{5}{3}$s or $\frac{6}{3}$s (the descending 5–6)
4.   A2 (D3/A4) (the ascending 5–6 technique)

A.

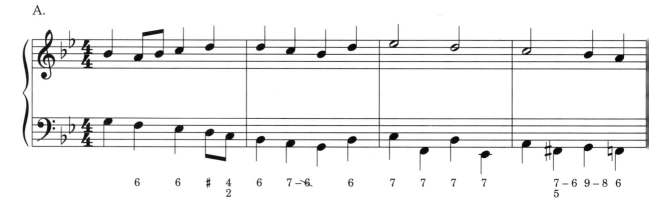

6   6   ♯ 4   6   7–6   6   7   7   7   7   7–6 9–8 6
                      2   5

B.

EXERCISE 20.3   Completion of Sequence Patterns

Write at least two repetitions of the sequence models given below. Lead each sequence to an authentic cadence. Analyze. Then, rewrite each completed sequence by adding at least one tone of figuration (e.g., suspension, passing tone) to the model and its copies.

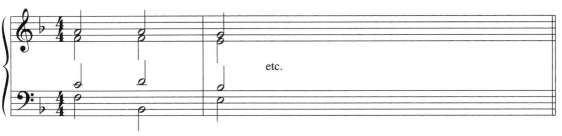

(Continued)

(*Continued*)

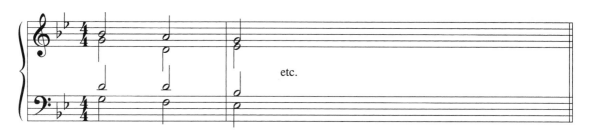

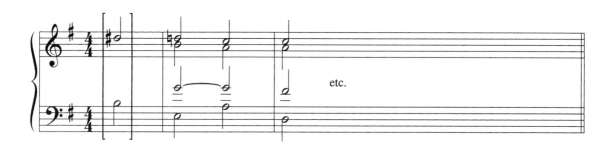

EXERCISE 20.4   Illustrations

Complete the following tasks in four-voice SATB style.

A. In D minor, write a four-measure phrase that includes the following:

  1. a D2 (D5/A4) sequence leading to an HC
  2. at least three suspensions
  3. a neighboring and cadential $^6_4$ chord

B. In B♭ major, write a four-measure phrase that includes the following:

  1. a contrapuntal expansion of tonic
  2. a D3 (D4/A2) sequence
  3. a bass suspension
  4. a bass arpeggiation
  5. a submediant harmony
  6. a deceptive progression

C. In C minor, write a four-measure phrase that includes the following:

  1. a D2 (D5/A4) sequence with interlocking sevenths
  2. passing tones

D. In A major, write a four-measure phrase that includes the following:

  1. an A2 (D3/A4) sequence (ascending 5–6)
  2. a deceptive progression
  3. two suspensions
  4. a neighboring $^6_4$ chord

EXERCISE 20.5   Analysis and Notation

The following sequences from the literature are missing bass lines. Listen to and study each sequence; then, identify each sequence and notate the bass line. Example G contains more than one sequence.

A. Mozart, *Allegro,* Piano Sonata in F Major, K. 332

Consider this excerpt to be in C minor. What rhythmic device is employed in mm. 64 and 65?

B. Chopin, Etude in G♭ major, op. 25

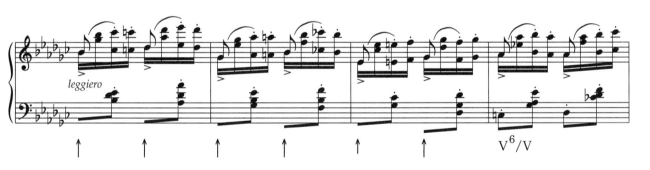

C. Haydn, *Moderato,* Piano Sonata No. 44 in B♭ major, Hob. XVI. 29

D.   Geminiani, *Violin Sonata*, op. 1, No. 12

E.   Bach, *Allemande*, English Suite No. 3 in G minor, BWV 808

F.   Corelli, *Allegro*, Concerto Grosso in F major, op. 6, no. 2

G. Tchaikovsky, Andantino in mododi canzona, Symphony No. 4

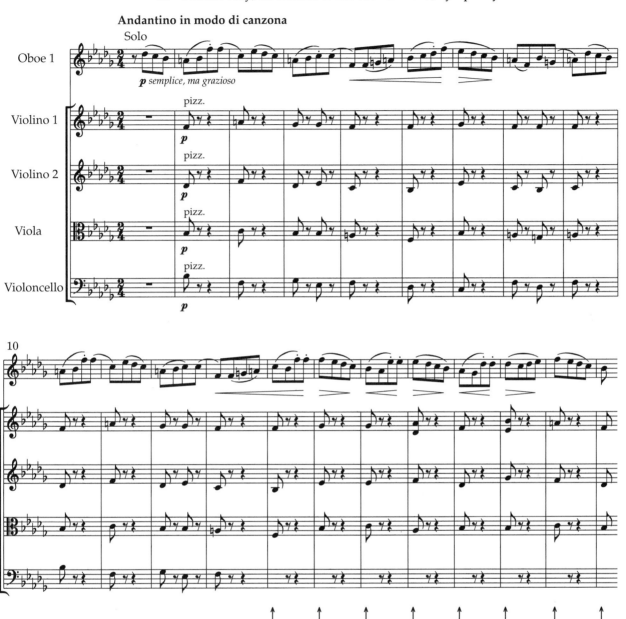

H. Corelli, *Gigue: Allegro*, Concerto Grosso in F major, op. 6, no. 12

(Continued)

(*Continued*)

EXERCISE 20.6   Notation of Sequences

You will hear several D2 (D5/A4) sequences with and without sevenths. You are to do the following:

1. determine whether the sequence contains alternating or interlocking sevenths
2. notate the bass

A.

B.

C.

D.   Handel: "Pena tiranna io sento" from *Amadigi di gaula*; act 1

E.   Bach, *Menuet II*, French Suite in D minor, BWV 812.
Measures 1–8 contain a sequential harmonic progression. Do not notate the bass for these measures; merely identify the sequential progression. Measures 9–16 are strictly sequential; notate the primary bass note in each measure. What is the harmonic relationship between the first and second eight-measure units?

F.   Schumann, "Ich will meine Seele tauchen" ("I Want to Delve my Soul"), *Dichterliebe*, op. 48, no. 5.
You will hear the entire song, which is composed of two large phrases. Each phrase may in turn be divided into two subphrases. What type of larger musical structure do the two large phrases create? Each large phrase begins unusually with a pre-dominant harmony, ii$^{\emptyset}_7$, rather than the tonic.

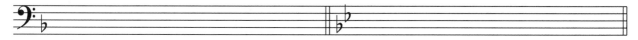

EXERCISE 20.7   Conversion

Reduce the excerpts below to homophonic four-voice textures. Then, convert the descending $^6_3$ passages into D2 (D5/A4) sequences with seventh chords. A worked solution appears below.

Sample Solution

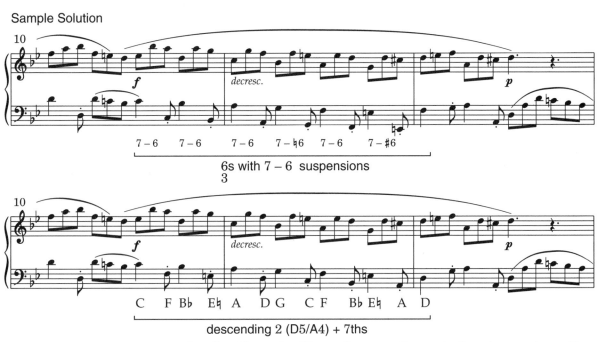

6s with 7 – 6 suspensions

3

descending 2 (D5/A4) + 7ths

A.   Corelli, *Allemanda: Allegro,* Concerto Grosso in C major, op. 6, no. 10

B.   Corelli, *Corrente,* Concerto Grosso in C major, op. 6, no. 10

C. Haydn, *Finale: Tempo di Minuet,* Piano Sonata No. 37 in E major, Hob. XVI. 22

EXERCISE 20.8   Analysis

Analyze the examples below that contain D2 (D5/A4) sequences with inverted seventh chords. Circle each chordal seventh and label its preparation and resolution.

A.   Leclair, *Sarabanda,* Trio Sonata in D major, op. 2, no. 8

B.   Marcello, *Largo,* Trio Sonata in B♭ major, op. 2, no. 2
Focus on the continuo realization.

EXERCISE 20.9   Figured Bass

Realize the figured bass below; bracket and label sequences. Provide a roman numeral analysis for all harmonies outside of the sequences. Inverted seventh chords must be complete.

EXERCISE 20.10   Comparison of Sequential Passages from the Literature

Below are three examples from Mozart's *Magic Flute*. Listen to each and then in a short paragraph, compare and contrast their content. Include in your discussion not only specific types of sequences but also their functions within the larger musical context.

Mozart's *Die Zauberflöte* (*The Magic Flute*), K. 620

A. "Drei Knäbchen" (Three Little Boys"), act I, scene 9

Drei Knäbchen, jung, schön, hold ,   Three boys, young, pretty, good,
    und weise   and wise
Umschweben euch auf eurer Reise.   Will hover near you on your journey.

B. "Holle Rache" ("Hell's Revenge"), act 2, scene 8

C.   "Wie, wie, wie?" ("What, What, What?"), act 2, scene 5

Wie, wie, wie?	What? What? What?
Ihr an diesem Schreckensort?	You in this place of dread?
Nie, nie, nie	Never, never, never
Kommt ihr wieder glücklich fort!	Will you come out again!

EXERCISE 20.11   Melody Harmonization and Sequences

Based on the contour of the following soprano fragments, determine an appropriate sequence type and then harmonize each in four voices (SATB). Examples A–D require one chord change for each melody note. Examples E–F contain tones of figuration and are incomplete. For these, determine the larger sequential pattern, add the sequential bass, and complete the sequence and lead to a cadence. Label each sequence type. A sample solution appears below.

(Continued)

(*Continued*)

A.

F *and* d

B.

a *and* C

C.

D.

E.

etc.

F.

etc.

EXERCISE 20.12   Analysis of Sequences Appearing in
Compound Melodies

 Determine the sequence type in the compound melodies below and then provide a reductive verticalization of the implied voices (either three or four).

Sample Solution

A2

D2

D2

A. Bach, *Menuet*, French Suite in B minor, BWV 814. Bracket subphrases in this example. What type of formal structure occurs?

B. Schumann, *Kreisleriana*, op. 16, no. 5
While not strictly a compound melody, it is possible to create a five-voice structure.

C. Bach, *Menuet*, French Suite in C minor, BWV 813

EXERCISE 20.13   Aural Identification of Sequences within Phrases

Notate the bass of the incomplete scores and provide a roman numeral analysis. Bracket and label sequences.

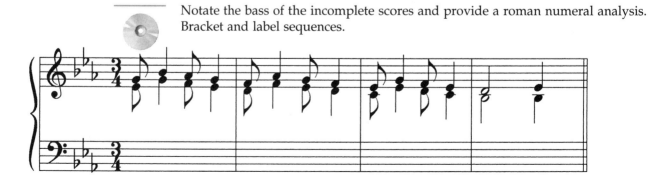

EXERCISE 20.14   Keyboard: Figured Bass

Realize the figured bass in four voices; a few given soprano pitches will guide your upper line. Sing the bass voice while playing the upper parts. Analyze.

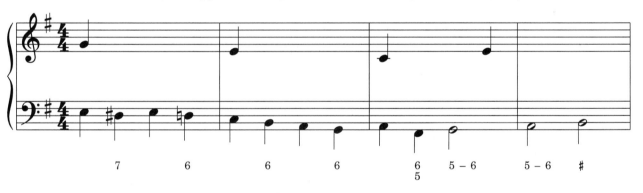

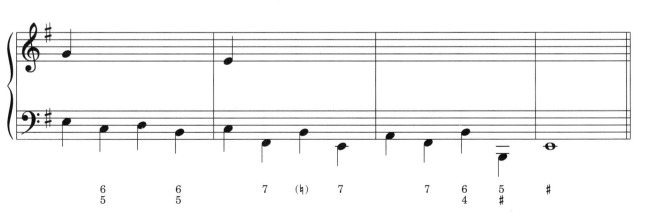

EXERCISE 20.15 Expansion of Basic Progressions

 You will hear two basic chord progressions; each is followed by elaborated versions that include contrapuntal expansions and sequences. Notate the bass and the soprano and include roman numerals. In a sentence or two, describe the way the tonic is expanded.

Model 1:

Expansion #1: (3 mm)   Expansion #2: (3 mm)

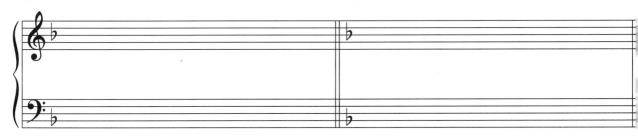

Expansion #3: (3 mm)   Expansion #4: (4 mm)

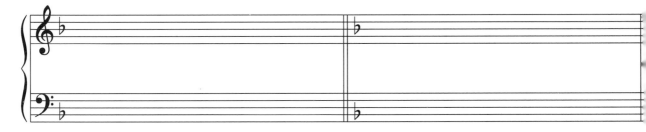

Model 2: (all expansions occupy four measures)

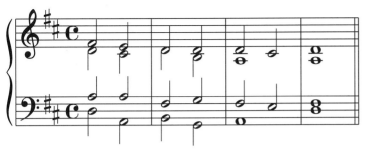

Expansion #1:

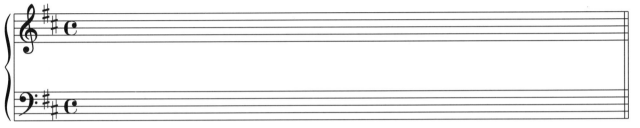

Expansion #2:

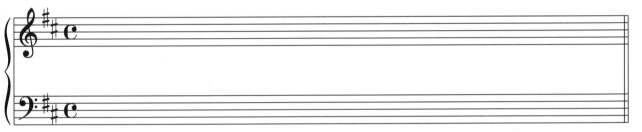

Expansion #3:

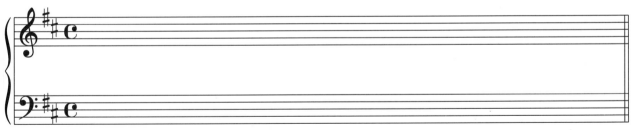

Expansion #4:

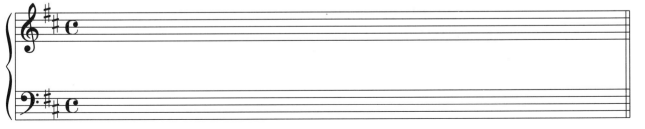

CHAPTER 21

Applied Chords

EXERCISE 21.1 Aural Comparison of Progressions with and without Applied Chords

You will hear four pairs of short progressions; the first progression of the pair is diatonic and the second adds applied chords that embellish the first progression. Listen to the model and write out the roman numerals. Then, listen to the second example, each of which contains one applied chord. For each applied chord you hear, write "V" beneath the harmony and follow it with an arrow that leads to the diatonic chord that is being tonicized. For example, if the first progression you hear is I–V–I, but the second contains an applied chord between the tonic and the dominant, you would write I–V–V–I.

A. model: ___ ___ ___

___ ___ ___ ___

B. model: ___ ___ ___ ___

___ ___ ___ ___ ___

C. model: ___ ___ ___

___ ___ ___ ___

D. model: ___ ___ ___ ___

___ ___ ___ ___ ___

EXERCISE 21.2 Recognizing Applied Chords: Analysis

The examples below contain applied chords: V(7)/ii, V(7)/III, V7/IV, V(7)/V, and V(7)/vi. All are possible in both major and minor keys except for V/ii in minor. Remember that dissonant triads such as iio cannot be tonicized. For each excerpt:

1. analyze all diatonic chords with roman numerals and give a second-level analysis.
2. circle and label each applied chord with a roman numeral.

A sample analysis has been given. Remember to use your eye and ear to pinpoint new chromatic tones and harmonies foreign to the key.

Mozart, *Trio*, String Quartet in E♭ major, K. 171

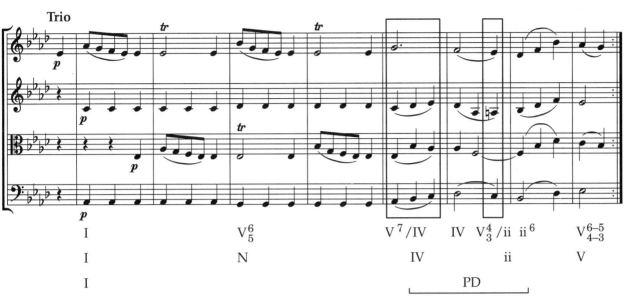

A.   B.

C.

D.

E.   Schubert, Waltz in B♭ major, *German Dances and Ecossaises*, D. 783

EXERCISE 21.3   Error Detection of Applied Chords

Below are notated and analyzed applied triads and Mm seventh chords. The last five examples include resolution of the applied chord.

Exercises A–E: Assume the roman numeral analysis and given key to be correct. Renotate incorrect pitches in each chord in order to conform to the roman numerals.

Exercises F–J: Assume the notated pitches and given key to be correct. Change incorrect roman numerals in order to conform to the notated pitches and given key.

Exercises K–O: Assume the roman numerals and given key to be correct. Renotate pitches in the applied chord and its resolution to conform to the analysis, the given key, and correct voice leading.

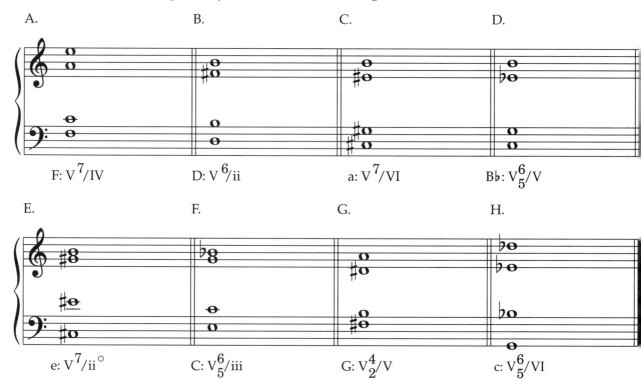

A.

B.

C.

D.

F: V⁷/IV   D: V⁶/ii   a: V⁷/VI   B♭: V⁶₅/V

E.

F.

G.

H.

e: V⁷/ii°   C: V⁶₅/iii   G: V⁴₂/V   c: V⁶₅/VI

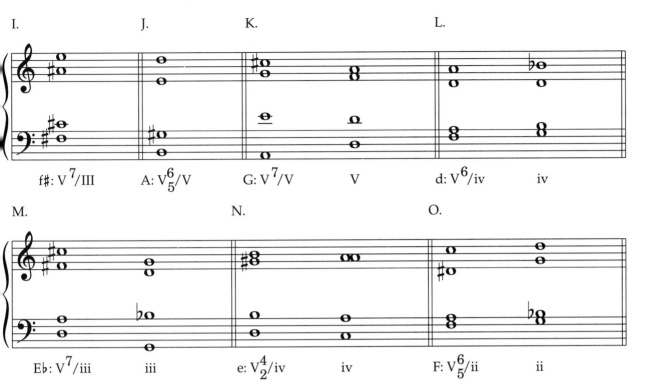

I.   J.   K.   L.

f#: V^7/III   A: V$^6_5$/V   G: V^7/V   V   d: V^6/iv   iv

M.   N.   O.

Eb: V^7/iii   iii   e: V$^4_2$/iv   iv   F: V$^6_5$/ii   ii

EXERCISE 21.4   Resolving Applied Chords

Analyze each applied chord according to the given key, then lead each to its respective tonic, resolving all tendency tones correctly. Example K is longer and requires you to notate both the applied chord and its resolution. Analyze.

A.   B.   C.

D: F: e:

D.   E.   F.

g: c: G:

d:

f#:

Eb:

Bb:

K.

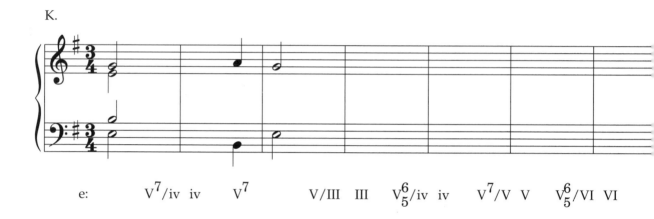

e: V^7/iv   iv   V^7 V/III   III   V$^6_5$/iv   iv   V^7/V   V   V$^6_5$/VI   VI

EXERCISE 21.5   Figured Bass with Given Soprano

The figured bass below incorporates applied chords. Fill in the inner voices and analyze using two levels.

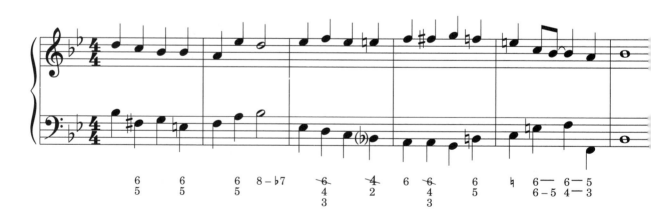

EXERCISE 21.6   Keyboard: Model Progressions

Play in major and minor modes as specified in keys up to and including two sharps and two flats. Be able to sing either outer voice while playing the remaining three voices. Analyze.

EXERCISE 21.7 Keyboard Brain Twister

Based on the given key signature determine the roman numeral for each given chord in both a major key and its relative minor. Then, play and resolve each applied chord. Finally, close each example with a cadence in the major key and the relative minor key.

EXERCISE 21.8 Figured Bass

Realize the figured basses that include applied vii°6 and vii°7 chords. The soprano is given. Provide a two-level analysis.

A.

B.

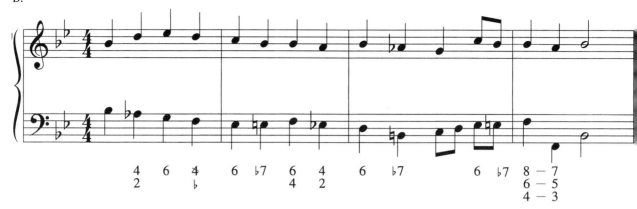

EXERCISE 21.9   Writing Applied vii°6 and vii°7

1. Complete the applied chords and resolve them, then compose an ending to the progression following the instructions preceding each example.
2. Provide a two-level analysis.

A.

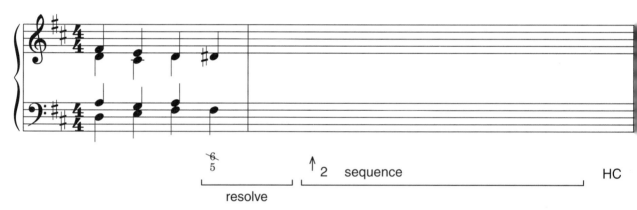

After resolving the applied chord, continue, using an A2 (D3/A4) + $\frac{6}{3}$ sequence (ascending 5–6 sequence) that leads to the dominant. Include two additional applied chords in this progression.

B.

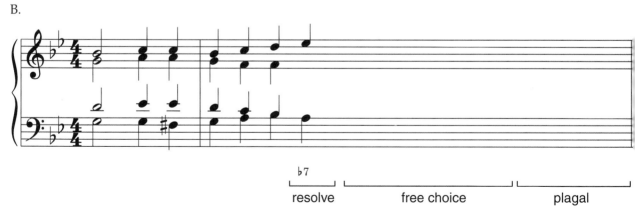

After resolving the applied chord, continue the progression for at least two measures using harmonies of your choice. There must be at least two added applied chords. Close with a plagal cadence.

C.

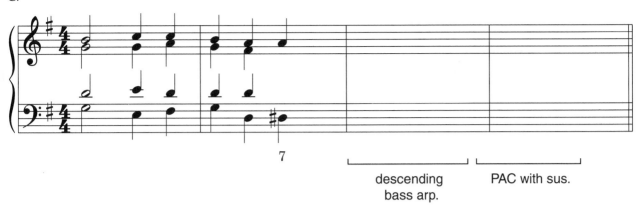

descending
bass arp.

PAC with sus.

After you resolve the applied chords, include a descending bass arpeggiation; close with a PAC that includes a suspension.

D.

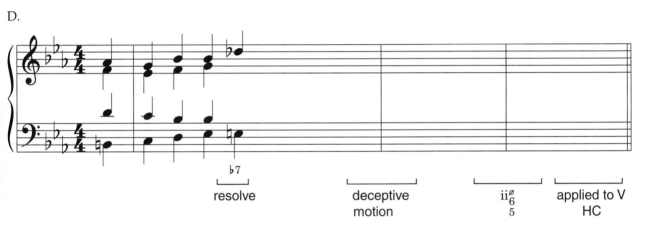

resolve

deceptive
motion

ii$^{\varnothing 6}_{5}$

applied to V
HC

After resolving the applied chord, include a deceptive harmonic motion followed by ii$^{\varnothing 6}_{5}$. Close with a half cadence; use an applied dominant seventh to precede the final dominant harmony.

EXERCISE 21.10 Keyboard: Short Progressions

Play the following progressions:

In G major and B♭ major: I–V$^6_5$/IV–IV
In G major and B♭ major: I–V7/ii–ii
In G major and B♭ major: V–V$^6_5$/vi–vi
In D major and F major: I–V$^4_3$/vi–vi–V$^6_5$/V–V
In A minor and E minor: i–V$^6_5$/III–III–V$^6_5$/iv–v–vii°7/V–V

EXERCISE 21.11 Notation of Chromatic Tones

Below are notated diatonic progressions, to which applied chords will be added. Notate appropriate pitches and roman numerals that reflect these added applied harmonies.

Listening tip: Remember, a chromatically raised pitch functions as the temporary leading tone to the next chord (i.e., it becomes $\hat{7}$), and a chromatically lowered pitch usually functions as the seventh of the chord that descends to the third of the following chord. The chromaticism often appears in an outer voice.

A.

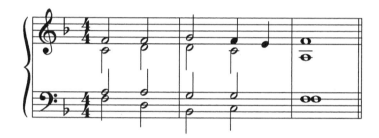

B.

C.   Note the parallel fifths between bass and tenor in m. 1. Recall that added applied chords are often used as voice-leading correctives that eliminate such fifths and octaves.

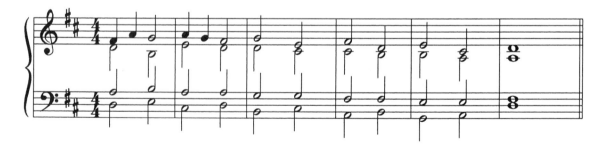

D.

E.

F.

EXERCISE 21.12 Analysis: Applied Chords within Phrases and Periods

Below are examples from the literature. Provide roman numerals (use two levels of analysis) and answer any questions on a separate piece of paper.

A. Beethoven, *Allegro* and *Adagio cantabile*, Piano Trio No. 1 in E♭ major, op. 1

1. In a sentence or two, discuss the phrase structure of the first passage. Is it a single phrase, a period, independent phrases, or some other structure?
2. Label the period type in the second excerpt.
3. Compare and contrast the harmonic structure of the two excerpts.

A1.

Note the $^6_4$ chord in m. 2; does it function as you would expect a $^6_4$ chord to function? (Hint: Is there an underlying progression in mm. 1 through 4?)

A2.

B.   Mozart, "Agnus Dei," *Requiem,* K. 626
     Do the chords in mm. 3 and 5 function harmonically or contrapuntally?

tol - - lis pec - ca - - ta mun - - di:

C. Mozart, *Allegro,* String Quartet in F major, K. 158

D.　Elgar, "Salut d'Amour" ("Love's Greeting"), op. 12
Make a phrase/period diagram.

E.　Haydn, *Allegro con spirito*, String Quartet in B♭ major, op. 76, no. 4, Hob. III. 78
Is this a single phrase or a period? Support your answer.

EXERCISE 21.13 Comparison of Applied Chords: Dominant Seventh Versus Diminished Seventh

 Differentiate between dominant seventh and diminished seventh applied chords. Then, notate the bass and the soprano voices and provide roman numerals.

A.   B.

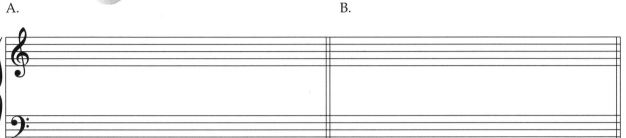

C.

D.   E.

EXERCISE 21.14 Figured Bass

Fill in the inner voices and analyze using two levels. Watch for added chromaticism.

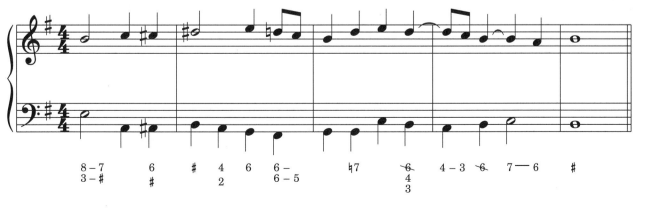

8 – 7   6   #   4   6   6 –   ♮7   6   4 – 3   6   7 — 6   #
3 – #   #   2   6 – 5   4
                                                3

EXERCISE 21.15   Harmonizing Melodic Fragments with Applied Chords

In a logical meter and rhythmic setting of your choice, harmonize the melodic fragments using applied chords. Arrows indicate applied chord placement. Your harmonic progression should make sense. Analyze.

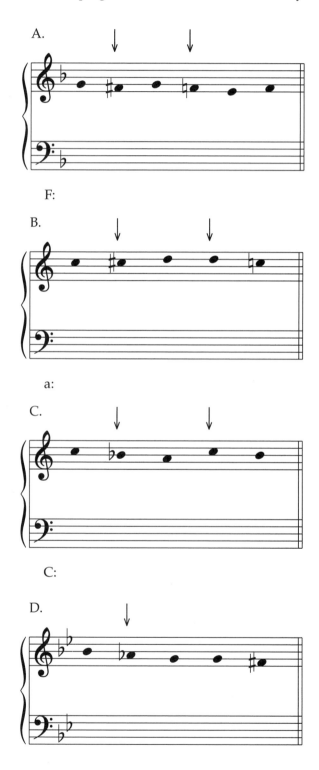

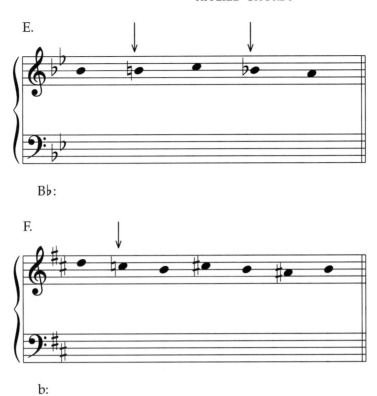

E.

Bb:

F.

b:

EXERCISE 21.16   Figured Bass

Write a soprano line and inner voices, and analyze using two levels.

A.

B.

(Continued)

(*Continued*)

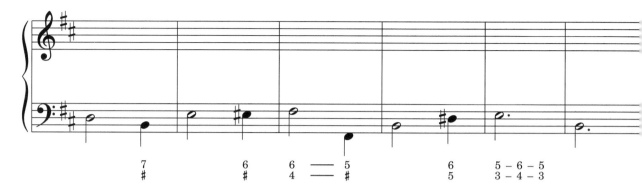

7   6   6 ——— 5   6   5 – 6 – 5
4 ——— #   5   3 – 4 – 3

EXERCISE 21.17   Keyboard: Figured Bass

Realize the figured bass below. Add inner voices and analyze with two levels.

7   6   ♮7   6   4   6   6   6 —— 5
#5   ♮5   5   2   ♮5   4 —— 3
#   #

EXERCISE 21.18   Writing Phrases, Periods, and Sentences

Construct periods in four voices based on the instructions below. Analyze and label each of the required elements.

A. In G major, write an eight-measure parallel interrupted period that contains the following:

1. at least two applied chords in its first phrase
2. at least two suspensions in its second phrase
3. one example of a neighboring, cadential, and passing $^6_4$ chord in one of the two phrases

B. In B minor, write an eight-measure parallel interrupted period that contains the following:

1. one D3 (D4/A2) sequence (may include the $^6_3$ form)
2. a bass suspension and at least three passing tones
3. two examples of applied diminished seventh chords in one of the two phrases

C. In G minor, write an eight-measure parallel sectional period that contains the following:

1. any sequence
2. an inverted applied dominant seventh chord
3. a cadential $^6_4$
4. two accented passing tones

D. In C minor, write an eight-measure sentence that contains the following:

1. a step-descent bass
2. an ascending bass arpeggiation
3. two examples of applied diminished seventh chords

E. In E♭ major, write an eight-measure contrasting continuous period that contains the following:

1. an A2 (D4/A3) sequence (or its $^6_3$ variant)
2. a deceptive progression
3. a suspension, accented passing tone, appoggiatura, and neighbor
4. a descending bass arpeggiation

EXERCISE 21.19 Analysis: Identification of Applied Chord Sequences

 Listen to and analyze each excerpt, marking the beginning and ending points of each sequence. Next, identify the sequence type by label. Finally, provide roman numerals for the remaining chords in each example.

A.

B.

C.

D.

E. Vivaldi, *Allegro,* Concerto Grosso in F major, op. 9, no. 11, Ry198A, Fi133, F.I/58, P416

EXERCISE 21.20   Applied Chord Sequences within the Phrase Model: Analysis and Notation

 You will hear four phrases from the literature that contain applied chord sequences. The upper voices are provided.

1. Identify the sequence and notate the bass line.
2. Provide a two-level analysis of the excerpt.

A. Mozart, *Minuetto,* String Quartet in B♭ major ("Hunt"), K. 458

B. Schubert, Waltz in G major, *Twelve German Dances and Five Ecossaises*, D. 529, no. 3

C. Schubert, Waltz in A major, *Twelve German Dances and Five Ecossaises*, D. 420, no. 12

D. Beethoven, *Adagio molto expressivo*, Violin Sonata No. 6 in A major, op. 30, no. 1
Note that there is a slightly longer tonicization of each step within the sequence.

EXERCISE 21.21   Completing Applied Chord Sequences

Determine the type of applied chord sequence, then continue the sequence and cadence. Begin by writing the diatonic chords, then insert the appropriate preceding applied chord.

A.

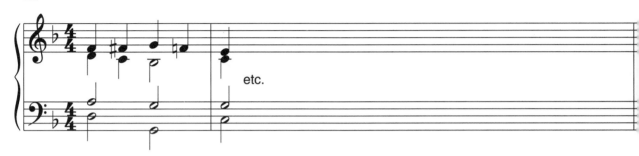

B.

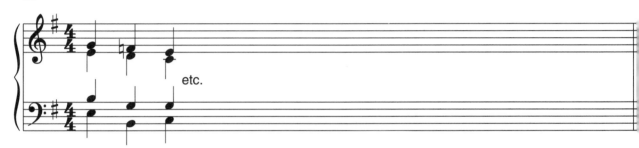

C.

D.

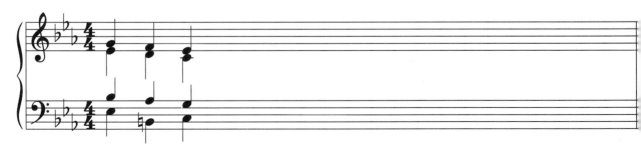

E.

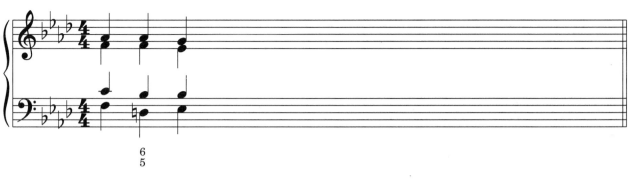

F.

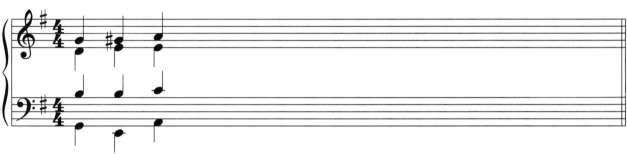

EXERCISE 21.22   Figured Bass

The figured bass below includes at least one applied chord sequence or sequential progression. Add roman numerals and inner voices.

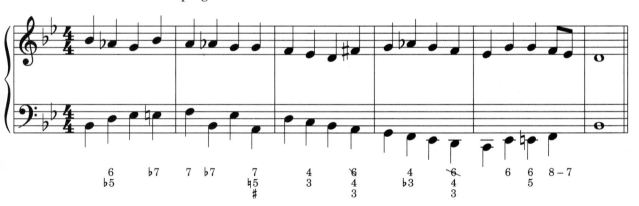

EXERCISE 21.23   Harmonizing Bass Lines

Harmonize each bass line below, which implies a diatonic or applied chord sequence. Determine a suitable meter; you may choose the note values. Analyze.

A.

F:

B.

A:

C.

b:

D.

c:

EXERCISE 21.24   Notation of Applied Chord Sequences

Add the missing bass voice using your ear and the visual clues provided by the given upper voices. Label the sequence type.

A.

B.

C.

D.

E.

EXERCISE 21.25   Figured Bass

The figured basses below (without soprano) include multiple applied chord sequences. Write a soprano voice, analyze, and add inner voices.

1.

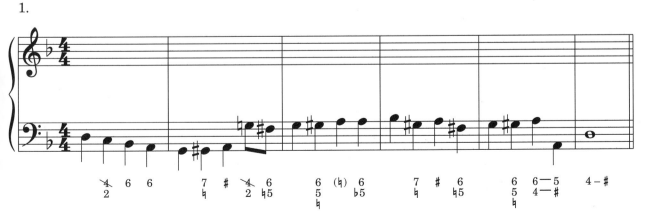

2.

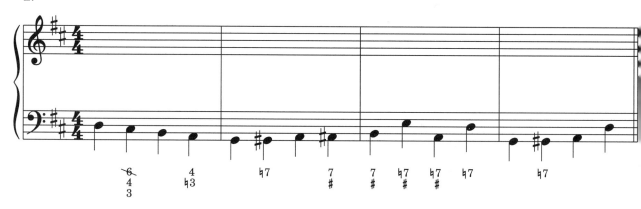

EXERCISE 21.26   Illustrations

Complete the tasks below in four voices; analyze.

A.   In C minor, write a D3 (D4/A2) sequence that incorporates root-position applied diminished seventh chords. Close with a PAC.

B.   In A major, write an A2 (D3/A4) with $^6_3$s with applied chords and an applied D2 (D5/A4) sequence with 7ths (interlocking or alternating). Close with an IAC.

C.   In G major, write a parallel interrupted period that includes the following:

1.   any applied chord sequence
2.   a deceptive progression
3.   two suspensions

D.   In B minor, write a progression that includes the following, but not necessarily in that order:

1.   an IAC
2.   an applied chord D2 (D5/A4) sequence using dominant seventh chords (alternating or interlocking)
3.   a neighboring and passing $^6_4$ chord
4.   a phrygian cadence
5.   a bass suspension
6.   a tonic expansion

EXERCISE 21.27   Keyboard: Unfigured Bass

Realize the unfigured bass in four voices. Write in a two-level analysis. Sing either outer voice while playing the other three.

CHAPTER 22

Tonicization and Modulation

EXERCISE 22.1   Analysis

Below are excerpts from the literature in which a nontonic harmony is expanded through tonicization. You are to do the following:

1. Listen to each phrase and bracket the expanded harmony.
2. Provide a detailed, chord-by-chord analysis of the harmonies within the expansion.
3. Provide a second-level analysis that places the tonicized area within the overall harmonic progression of the entire passage.

A.   Mendelssohn, *Allegro arioso,* Cello Sonata No. 1 in B♭ major, op. 45

B1, 2. Corelli, *Adagio,* Concerto Grosso, op. 6, nos. 9 and 11
Below are two *Adagio* sections from two Corelli concertos. Analyze and in a short paragraph, compare and contrast their harmonic content.

1.

2. Consider this example to be in G minor.

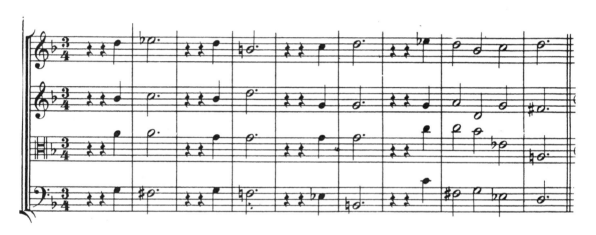

C. Schumann, "Du bist wie eine Blume" ("You Are So Like a Flower"), *Myrten*, op. 25, no. 24

Du bist wie eine Blume,   You are so like a flower,
So hold und schön und rein;   So pure, and fair, and kind,

D. Schumann, "Talismane," *Myrten*, op. 25, no. 8

Gottes ist der Orient!
dent! Nord - und süd - li-ches Ge-län-de ruht im Frie - den sei - ner Hän-de.

Gottes ist der Orient!	The Orient is God's!
Gottes ist der Occident!	The Occident is God's!
Nord und südliches Gelände	Northern and southern lands
Ruht im Frieden seiner Hände	Repose in the peace of His hands.

E. Schumann, *Mit feuer*, Piano Trio in D major, op. 63

(*Continued*)

(Continued)

F. Bellini, "Casta on Diva" from *Norma*, Act I, scene 4, cavatino

EXERCISE 22.2   Figured Bass and Tonicized Areas

In order to realize the figured basses, you will need to determine which non-tonic harmonies are extended. Begin by studying the bass and figures. The appearance of chromaticism in the figures and the bass will help you.

1. Bracket each tonicized area and represent its relation to the main tonic by using a roman numeral.
2. Add upper voices and a first-level roman numeral analysis that relates each of the chords within a tonicization to the expanded harmony.

EXERCISE 22.3   Soprano Harmonization

Harmonize each soprano fragment below in three different ways. Try to incorporate applied chords, diatonic and applied chord sequences, and tonicized areas. Begin by breaking up the melodies into harmonic cells.

A.

B.

C.

EXERCISE 22.4 Analysis of Tonicized Areas and Modulations

 The following progressions contain either tonicized areas (which close in their original key) or modulations (which close in a new key, though they may also contain tonicized areas). Use brackets to identify tonicized areas, with the roman numeral of the temporary tonal area shown below the bracket. Identify a single underlying tonal progression in examples that contain tonicized areas. Use pivots to show modulations (modulations in this exercise—though they contain pivots and demonstrate closure in a new tonal area—are artificial, given their necessary brevity). Analyze each example with two levels of roman numerals.

A.

B.

C. Beethoven, *Mit Lebhaftigkeit und durchaus mit Empfindung und Ausdruck,* Piano Sonata No. 27 in E minor, op. 90

Mit Lebhaftigkeit und durchaus mit-Empfindung und Ausdruck.*

D.

E.   Schubert, Ballet music from *Rosamunde*, D. 797

EXERCISE 22.5   Key Choices

List the closely related keys to each of the given keys. Review the various ways you can determine closely related keys.

D major __ __ __ __ __   F minor __ __ __ __ __

A♭ major __ __ __ __ __   C♯ minor __ __ __ __ __

B minor __ __ __ __ __   D♭ major __ __ __ __ __

B♭ major __ __ __ __ __

EXERCISE 22.6   Modulating Figured Basses

Realize the short figured basses below in four voices. Then analyze, being sure to label pivot chords fully.

A.

B.

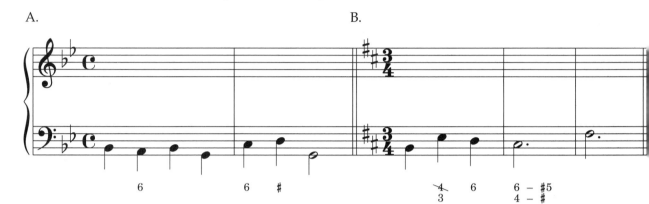

C.

D.

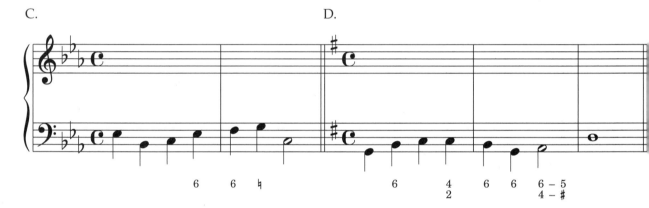

E.

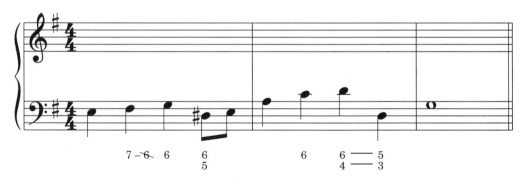

F.

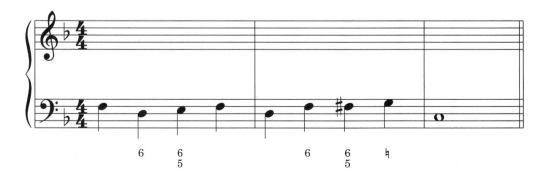

G.

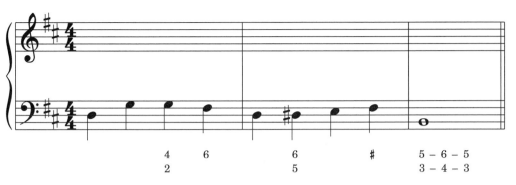

$$
\begin{array}{ccccc}
4 & 6 & 6 & \# & 5-6-5 \\
2 & & 5 & & 3-4-3
\end{array}
$$

H.

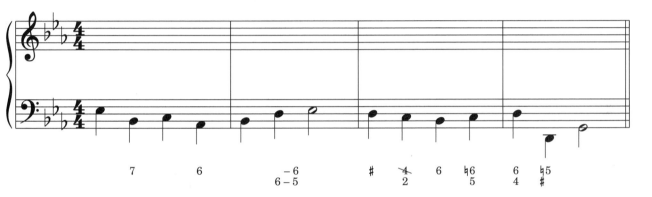

$$
\begin{array}{cccccccc}
7 & 6 & -6 & \# & \cancel{4} & 6 & \natural6 & 6 & \natural5 \\
& & 6-5 & & 2 & & 5 & 4 & \# \\
\end{array}
$$

EXERCISE 22.7   Keyboard: Multiple Tonal Destinations

Below is the opening of a phrase and its continuation that leads to three different keys. Play each progression and analyze.

1. Determine the relationship of the new key to the old key, using roman numerals.
2. Determine the pivot chord and box it, showing original and new keys.

EXERCISE 22.8   Keyboard: Modulating Sopranos

Determine the implied initial key and the new key of each soprano fragment. Accidentals will narrow your choices considerably, but it is possible that a diatonic melody modulates without accidentals; thus, there may be more than one harmonic interpretation. Write out the bass line of the cadence and the preceding pre-dominant. Determine a possible bass for the opening of the progression. You will most likely end up in the approximate middle of the fragment, and the one or two unharmonized soprano pitches will be your modulatory pivot. Analyze and add inner voices.

EXERCISE 22.9   Notation of Modulating Phrases and Pivot Chord Location

Each short progression modulates, closing with a PAC. Before listening, determine modulatory possibilities. This is important because successful development of aural and analytical skills depends not only on active processing of what is seen and heard, but also on knowledge of normative procedures, which develops musical expectations. By using expectations, the number of possibilities is greatly reduced and you can then focus on just a handful of logical solutions.

An incomplete score is given for each example. Add missing bass and soprano pitches and provide roman numerals; mark the pivot chord.

A.

B.

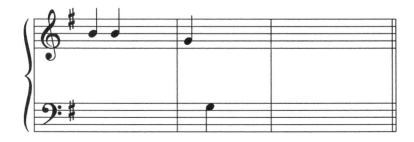

C.

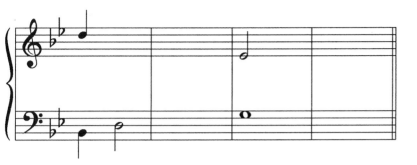

D.

E.

F.

EXERCISE 22.10   Keyboard: Improvising Modulating Consequents

Work out a modulating consequent phrase that continues musical ideas presented in the antecedent phrase. The result will be a parallel progressive period. After studying each of the three antecedent phrases, begin the consequent in the same way that the antecedent began, but you will insert a pivot chord approximately halfway through the consequent and cadence in the new key.

A. Emilie Zumsteeg, "Nachruf" ("Farewell"), op. 6, no. 6

1. Nur ei - ne laß von dei nen-Ga - ben, ver schwund-ne-Lie - be,_ mir_ zu - rück!

Nur eine lass von deinen Gaben,   Only leave one gift with me,
Verschwundne Liebe, mir zurück!   Vanished love, return to me!

B. Mozart, "Sehnsuch nach dem Frühlinge" ("Longing for Spring"), K. 596

Fröhlich

1. Komm, lie - ber Mai, und ma - che die Bäu - me wie - der grün,

Komm, lieber Mai, und mache   Come, dear May, and make
Die Baume wieder grün   the trees green again,

C. Clara Schumann, "Cavatina," *Variations de Concert sur la Cavatine du "Pirate" di Bellini*, op. 8

Andantino
molto espressivo

p

sempre piano il Basso.

EXERCISE 22.11 Dictation of Longer Modulating Phrases

Notate bass and soprano for Examples A–C and bass only for Examples D–K. Provide a roman numeral analysis and label the pivot chord.

A.

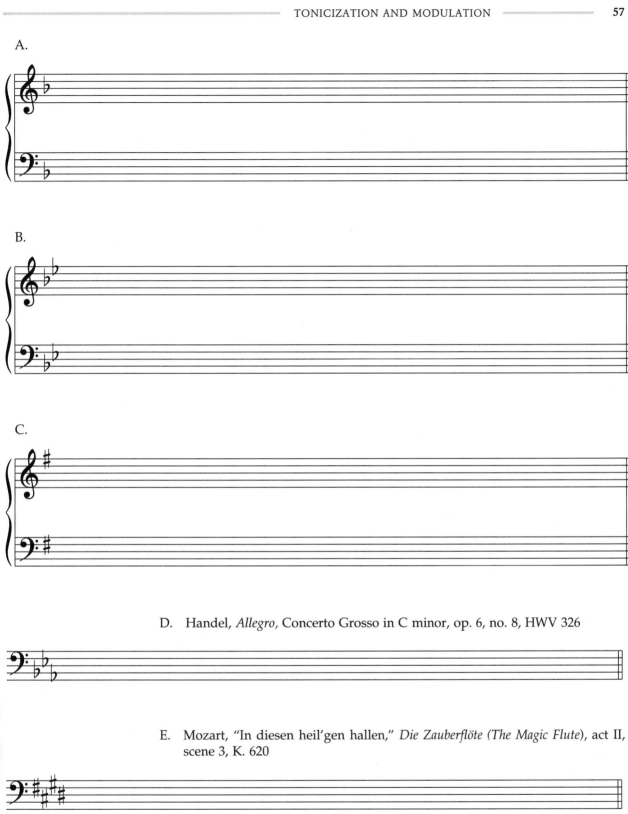

B.

C.

D.   Handel, *Allegro*, Concerto Grosso in C minor, op. 6, no. 8, HWV 326

E.   Mozart, "In diesen heil'gen hallen," *Die Zauberflöte (The Magic Flute)*, act II, scene 3, K. 620

F.   Haydn, *Adagio*, String Quartet in C major, op. 54, no. 2, Hob. III. 58

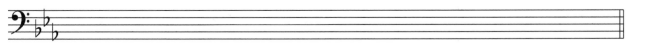

G.   Schubert, Waltz in B minor, *38 Waltzes, Ländler, and Ecossaises*, D. 145

H.   Beethoven, *Lustig-Traurig*, WoO 54

I.   Haydn, *Allegro,* String Quartet in F major, op. 74, no. 2, Hob. III. 70

J.   Chopin, Mazurka in A minor, op. 7, no. 2, BI 61

K.   Haydn, *Trio*, Piano Sonata in C major, Hob. XVI. 10

EXERCISE 22.12   Figured Bass

Add upper voices to the figured basses below, each of which modulates by sequence.

A.

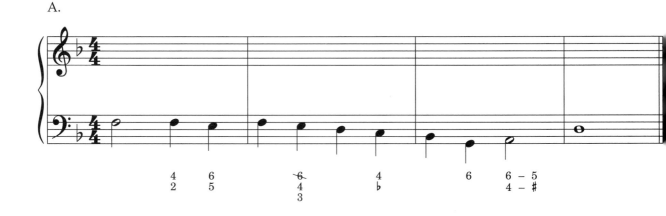

B.

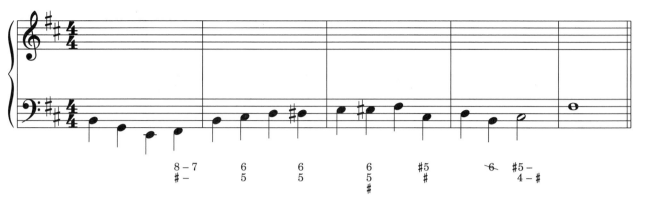

8 – 7   6   6   6   #5   -6-   #5 –
–   5   5   5   #   4 –
                          #

EXERCISE 22.13   Writing Modulating Sequences

Complete the following ordered tasks.

A.   Write a progression that

1.   establishes F major.
2.   incorporates a diatonic D2(D5/A4) sequence that breaks off early and becomes a pivot leading to the new key of vi.
3.   establishes the key of vi.

B.   Write a progression in C minor that modulates to III using an A2 (D3/A4) sequence; cadence in the new key.

C.   Write a progression in B minor that modulates to iv using a D2 (D5/A4) sequence with applied chords; cadence in the new key.

D.   Write a progression that

1.   establishes A major using a descending bass arpeggiation.
2.   modulates to iii using any sequence you wish.
3.   establishes iii with a step-descent bass.
4.   cadences in iii.

EXERCISE 22.14   Dictation: Variations of a Structural Progression

Study the model below, then listen to and notate the bass and soprano voices, and provide roman numerals for the following elaborations of the model. Modulations to closely related keys will occur. Label pivot chords.

Model A

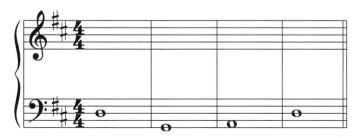

1.   2.

3.   4.

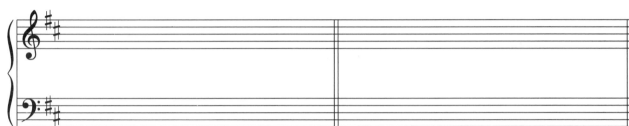

5.

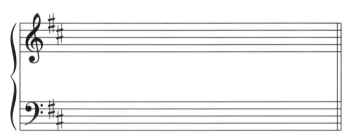

Model B

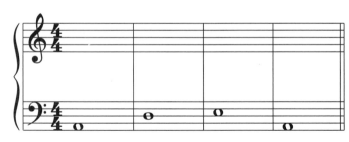

PD

1.   2.

3. 4.

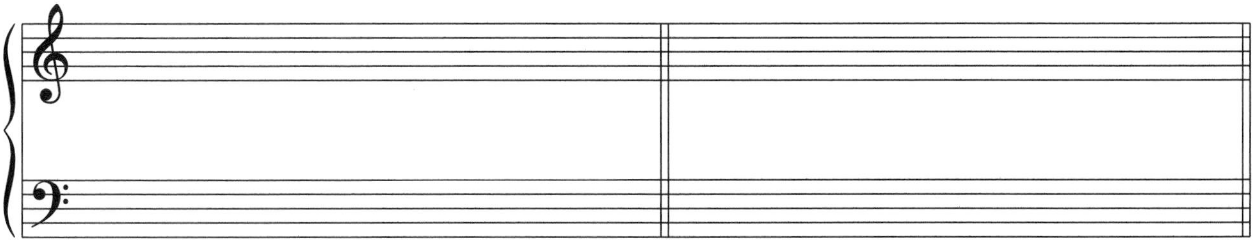

5.

Model C

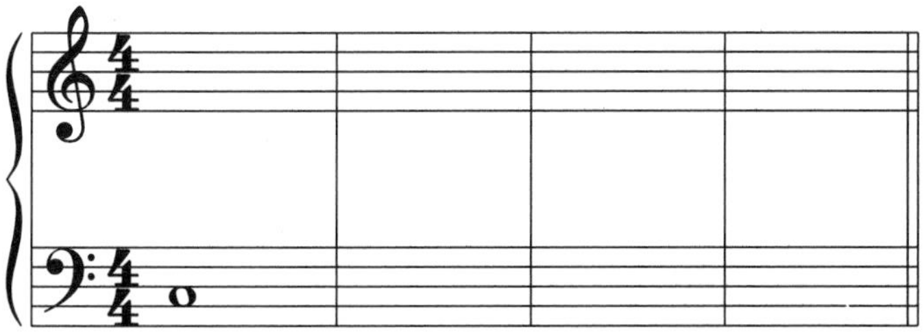

PD   V   I / i

1. 2.

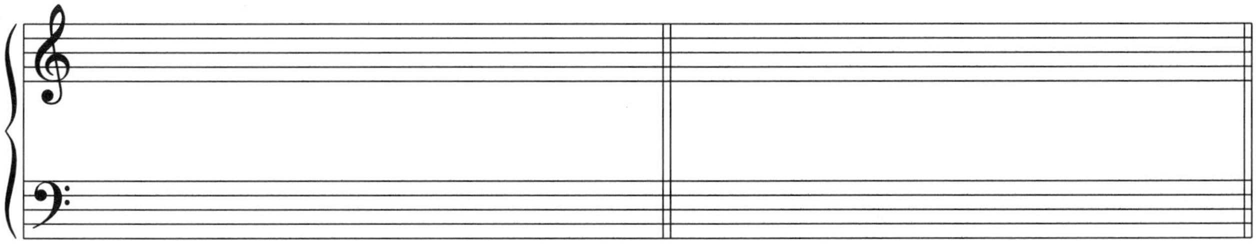

3. 4.

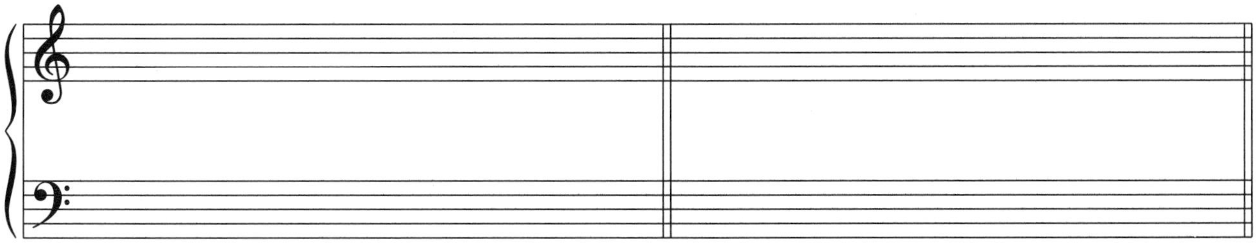

5.   6.

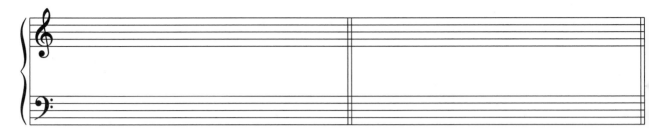

Model C

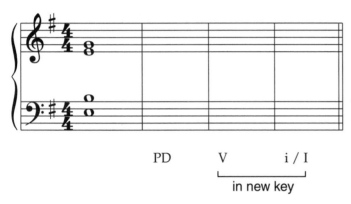

PD   V   i / I
            └─────────┘
             in new key

1.   2.

3.   4.

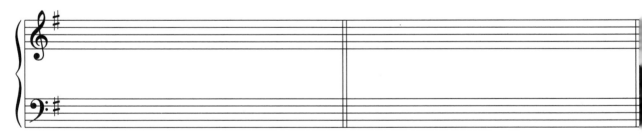

5.

EXERCISE 22.15   Composition

A.   Analyze the antecedent phrase below using roman numerals and figured bass; label tones of figuration and figured bass. Then, write three different consequent phrases to the antecedent, creating the following three period types: PIP, CIP, and PPP (you may close in either v or III).

B.   Analyze the chord progression in the first four measures of the example below. This will become the accompaniment for a melody that you will write. Then, in four voices, realize the figured bass that concludes the first phrase. Write a second phrase that modulates to and closes in a new key of your choice. Finally, write a suitable melody for both phrases.

CHAPTER 23

Binary Form and Variations

EXERCISE 23.1   Analysis

It is now your turn to analyze. Study each score, provide a formal diagram and label, and answer the accompanying questions.

A.   Haydn, String Quartet in G major, op. 33, no. 1, Scherzando

B. Türk, *Evening Song*

What type of period opens the piece (mm. 1–8)?

C. Haydn, *Menuet al rovescio*, Piano Sonata No. 41 in A Major, Hob. XVI. 26

1. What is the form?
2. Even though none of the material returns literally, there is a sense that you've heard it all before. Haydn has entitled this movement a "menuet in reverse." Describe what this means (hint: compare the end of A with the beginning of the digression).

MENUET AL ROVESCIO

*)

(Continued)

(Continued)

D. Bach, *Sarabande,* Lute Suite No. 3 in A minor, BWV 995

1. What is the form?
2. What is the overall tonal structure?

E. François Couperin, *Menuet,* Concerts Royaux, No. 1 in G major for flute, oboe, and basso continuo

The basso continuo, which is written in the lower two staves, comprises two instruments: harpsichord and cello (originally viola da gamba). Thus, even though this is referred to as a trio, there are four players.

1. What is the form?
2. There are many melodic relationships between the instruments.
    a. What is the relationship between the opening winds and the continuo in mm. 1–2? Be specific.
    b. The continuo repeats the winds' material once literally and once in augmentation in the A section. Label these spots.
    c. In the digression, Couperin develops and intensifies the relationships between the instruments. For example, the descending tune is an inversion

of the menuet's opening tune, and imitation and pairing of voices occur between all instruments. Find two or three instances of such repetitions.

3. What single key controls mm. 9–16?
4. What is the large-scale tonal progression in mm. 1–20?

F. Kirnberger, Lullaby

There are no repeat signs, but one could say that this piece conforms to the
two-reprise binary-form idea. Determine a logical place to add the repeat signs.
What type of binary form results? Give two or three reasons why you put
the repeats where you did. What harmonic procedure is used in mm. 9–12? Be
specific.

G. Fischer, "Uranie: Sarabande," *Musicalischer Parnassus*

Discuss the overall tonal progression in this piece. Is the D minor harmony that
occurs in m. 17 or in m. 22 the true tonal return? What harmonic technique opens
the piece? How would you interpret the cadence in m. 8 in terms of the large-
scale tonal progression of the piece? Label and discuss any later appearances of
this technique.

H.   Robert Schumann, Romance in B♭ minor, *Three Romances,* op. 28, no. 1

1.   Analyze mm 1–8, determining the overall harmonic progression.
2.   Label any sequences
3.   C major is extended from m. 13 to the downbeat of m. 16. What is its harmonic function?

(Continued)

(*Continued*)

I. Galuppi, Sonata in D major, Adagio

To determine the form, consider the unusual proportions in the piece: the material after the first double bar occupies fewer measures than the material before the first double bar.

EXERCISE 23.2 Analysis and Notation

Trio from Beethoven's Piano Trio No. 8, op. 38 (adapted from the Septet, op. 20)
Notate the missing left-hand pitches. Provide a two-level harmonic analysis. Determine the form. What proportional structure does Beethoven employ in mm. 1–8?

(Continued)

(*Continued*)

EXERCISE 23.3   Aural Analysis

We now analyze without the scores. Begin by studying the questions that accompany each piece. For each piece, provide a complete formal label.

A.   Beethoven, "Traurig," *Lustig-Traurig*, WoO 54

This short piece is in C minor, in $\frac{3}{8}$ meter. Repeat signs are observed.

1.   What type of period occurs in the A section?
2.   Notate the bass line of the first four measures on the staff below. You need notate only the "harmonic" (lowest) note of the Alberti figure, which occurs on each measure's downbeat.

B.   Purcell, "Ah! How Pleasant 'tis to Love," Z. 353

This piece is in C major, $\frac{3}{4}$ meter.

1.   Notate the opening melody of the piece (mm. 1–8) below with pitch and rhythm (begin by parsing it into phrases).
2.   The upper part of the second section of the piece is given below; notate the bass line and provide a roman numeral analysis.

C. Haydn, *Menuetto,* Piano Sonata in A major, Hob. XVI. 12
This *Menuetto* is in A major, $\frac{3}{4}$ meter.

1. How many phrases are there in the first section (up to the first major cadence)? What are their lengths? Discuss any unusual proportions.
2. Is the melodic material that begins the digression new? If not, from where is it derived?

D. Loeillet, *Largo,* Trio Sonata for two violins and continuo, op. 2, no. 9
This slow movement is in G minor, $\frac{3}{4}$ meter.

1. What key is tonicized at the first double bar?
2. There are two phrases in mm. 1 to 8. Do they form a period? If so, what type?
3. Notate the bass line of mm. 1 to 8 and provide roman numerals. Focus on one phrase at a time, memorizing its entire harmonic progression.

4. Label the sequences in the second half of the piece in their order of appearance.
5. Are any new keys tonicized in the second half of the piece? If so, what are they?
6. At what point does the tonic return in the second part of the piece?

E. Mozart, *Menuetto,* String Quartet No. 11 in E♭ major, K. 171
This movement is in E♭ major, $\frac{3}{4}$ meter.

1. To what key does the first section modulate?
2. Notate the bass line and provide roman numerals for mm. 1–4 on the staff below.

3. What contrapuntal technique characterizes the digression?
4. What harmony is prolonged in the digression?

F. Schubert, *Trio,* Sonatina for Piano and Violin in G minor, op. posth. 127, no. 3, D. 408
This movement is in E♭ major, $\frac{3}{4}$ meter.

1. Notate the bass line for mm. 1 to 8 and provide roman numerals.

2. Notate the bass line for the digression and provide roman numerals (the starting pitch is G). What harmonic procedure governs the harmony in this section?

3. Finally, notate the rest of the piece (eight measures). You have now notated the harmonic structure for an entire movement; congratulations.

EXERCISE 23.4   Analysis of Variation Excerpts

Below are complete themes and opening passages of two or three of their following variations. Study each theme and its variations in order to determine whether the variation set is continuous or sectional and what musical elements (for example, harmony, figuration, etc.) remain fixed (or only minimally changed) and what elements are varied. If the theme is sectional, label its overall form (except for Example B). Begin by providing roman numerals for the theme and studying the melody. Then, work through each variation, focusing on the varied element. Circle the original components of the melody in order to see exactly how the composer has altered it in the variations.

A.   Handel, *Gavotte: Allegro*, Keyboard Suite XIV in G major, HWV 222

Variation 2

B.   Handel, *Air*, Keyboard Suite III in D minor, HWV 104

(Continued)

(*Continued*)

1. Variation

2. Variation

3. Variation

C. Schubert, Impromptu in B♭ major, *Four Impromptus for Piano*, op. posth. 142, no. 3, D. 935

(Continued)

(Continued)

D.   Mozart, *Andantino cantabile*, Violin Sonata in G major, K. 379

(Continued)

(*Continued*)

EXERCISE 23.5 Composition (I)

Below are complete themes or portions of themes, followed by the openings of two or three of their variations. Analyze the theme, then complete each variation by continuing its initial texture and accompanimental patterns. For Example A, lead each variation to a cadence in the dominant.

A. Fischer, "Euterpe," *Musicalischer Parnassus*

THEME

Var. 1

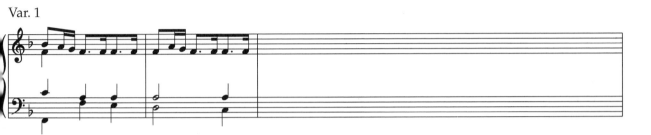

Var. 2

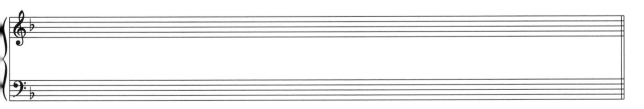

(Continued)

(Continued)

Var. 3

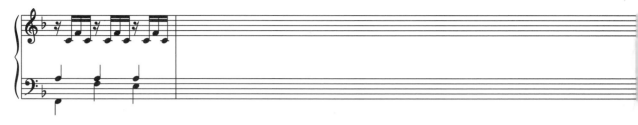

B.   Mozart, "Thema, Var. I, Var II, and Var. VII," *Variations on "La bergere Celimene"* for Violin and Piano, K. 359.

THEME   **Allegretto**

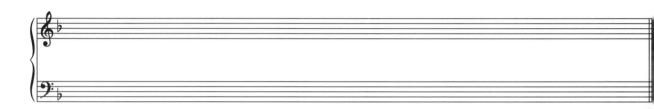

VAR. II

VAR. VII
Minore

EXERCISE 23.6 Composition (II)

Study the themes below, then write two or three variations on each.

A. Fischer, "Uranie," *Musicalischer Parnassus*

B. Haydn, *Tempo di Menuet*, Piano Sonata No. 34 in D major, Hob. XVI. 33

EXERCISE 23.7 Keyboard: Aria Pastorella

This assignment gives you an opportunity to flex your compositional muscles by creating a small binary piece. Given is the first phrase, which sets the mood and provides you with a model from which the rest of your composition will flow. Think of this binary as a motion to the mediant in m. 8 followed by a drive to the dominant and the subsequent harmonic interruption. The next section (mm. 13–16) remains entirely in the tonic. Begin by determining the harmonic structure. Measures 1–8 are subdivided into two phrases. You might begin the second phrase in the tonic, but think about moving toward the mediant about halfway through in order to prepare the cadence in III in m. 8. The material after the double bar might be sequential, leading to the structural dominant. Consider a restatement of the opening material for the final bars, which will create a rounded form and save you time composing new material. Play your solution in four voices, keyboard style. Feel free to include various tones of figuration. You may even wish to figurate your piece using an accompanimental texture beneath a tune.

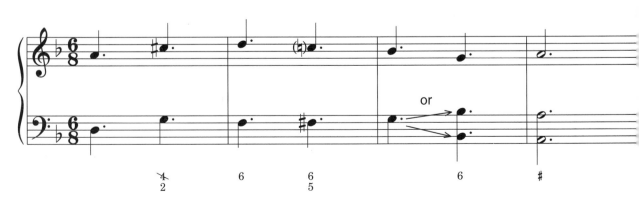

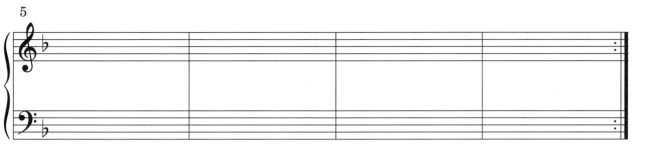

-------→ III

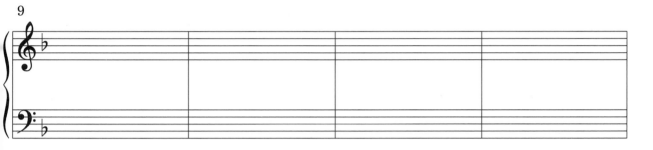

-------→ V

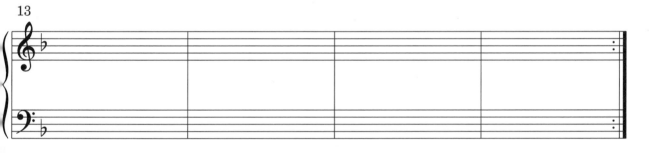

i   i

EXERCISE 23.8   Composition (III)

Complete the tasks below.

A.   Analyze the antecedent phrase below, then write a consequent phrase, which eventually returns to tonic. Add a melody for any solo instrument or voice.

B.   Analyze the antecedent phrase below, then write a consequent that modulates to III. Include repeat signs at the beginning of the antecedent and the end of the consequent. Write a melody for both phrases that contains a recurring rhythmic or pitch motive. Write another passage of approximately six to eight measures that is sequential and leads to the dominant. Finally, restate the opening eight-measure period, but rewrite the last phrase so that it closes on the tonic. You should end up with a rounded continuous binary form.

CHAPTER 24

Modal Mixture

EXERCISE 24.1   Analysis

Determine the locations and types of mixture harmonies in the excerpts from the literature. Be aware that not all chromatically altered chords result from mixture; some are applied chords. (Recall that mixture harmonies are independent chords that participate in the harmonic progression and usually carry a pre-dominant function. Applied harmonies, on the other hand, function exclusively as dominants, and they lead to their temporary tonics, to which they are subordinate.) Provide roman numerals for each chord. For mixture harmonies, circle chromatic pitches and label their scale degrees.

A. Mozart, *Allegro,* Clarinet Quintet in A major, K. 581
What melodic/contrapuntal function does the harmony in m. 4 serve?

(*Continued*)

(Continued)

E:

B. Mahler, "Die zwei blauen Augen von meinem Schatz" ("The Two Blue Eyes of My Darling"), *Lieder eines fahrenden Gesellen (Songs of a Wayfarer)*, no. 4
What is the mode of this excerpt? In spite of the pedal that runs through the entire excerpt, one can trace an implied progression of tonic–pre-dominant–dominant–tonic within the excerpt. Mark these functions.

Ich bin ausgegangen in stiller Nacht   I went out into the quiet night
Wohl über die dunkle Heide.   well across the dark heath.

C.   Beethoven, *Adagio sostenuto*, Violin Sonata No. 9 in A major, "Kreutzer," op. 47
Explore the possibility that Beethoven is introducing modal mixture in stages,
first melodically and then harmonically.

Adagio sostenuto

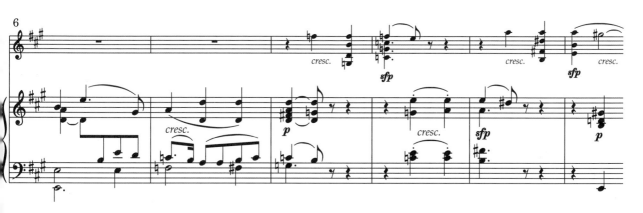

EXERCISE 24.2   Figured Bass

Realize in four voices and analyze.

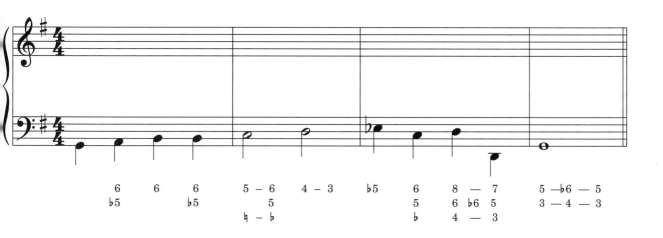

EXERCISE 24.3   Unfigured Bass

Based on the harmonic implications of the bass, determine a logical chord progression, add upper voices, and analyze. Include as many mixture harmonies as possible.

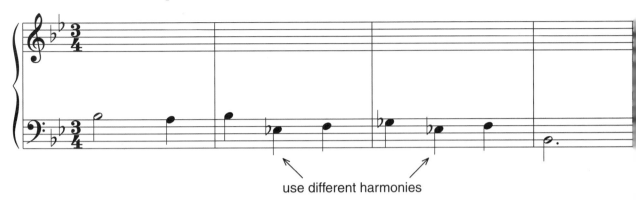

use different harmonies

EXERCISE 24.4   Melody Harmonization

Harmonize in four voices, adding as many mixture harmonies as possible. Analyze. Asterisks indicate potential mixture harmonies.

EXERCISE 24.5   Analytical and Aural Identification of Mixture: Correction

Listen to the recording, which contains numerous pitch differences from what is notated. Most of these differences occur on mixture harmonies. Correct the scores to conform to what is played. In addition, correct any spelling mistakes (including enharmonic errors). Analyze each progression below with roman numerals.

A.

B.

C.

D.

E.

EXERCISE 24.6   Keyboard: Figured Bass Review: Applied Chords

Realize the figured bass below in four voices. Analyze.

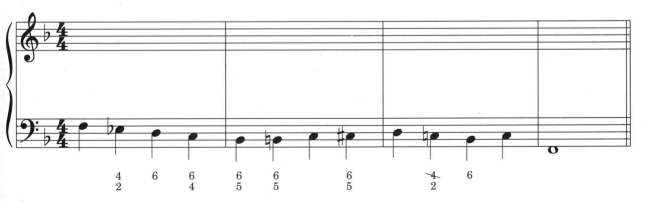

EXERCISE 24.7   Keyboard: Unfigured Bass Review of Tonicization and Modulation

Realize the following unfigured bass (with given soprano) in four voices. Be able to sing either given voice while playing the other three voices. Analyze.

EXERCISE 24.8   Keyboard: Figured Bass with Mixture

Realize the figured bass below in four voices. Analyze.

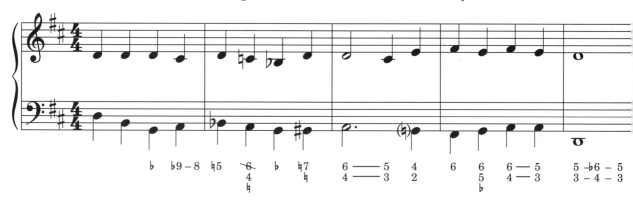

EXERCISE 24.9   Analysis

The examples below contain many types of modal mixture. Analyze each harmony with roman numerals and figured bass. Mixture choices include: minor tonic (i), diminished supertonic (ii°), half-diminished supertonic (ii⌀⁶₅, ii⌀⁴₃), lowered mediant (♭III), minor subdominant (iv₇), minor dominant (v), lowered submediant (♭VI), and various combinations of the above in the step-descent bass.

A.

B.

C.

D.   Beethoven, *Lebhaft. Marschmässig,* Piano Sonata No. 28 in A major, op. 101

EXERCISE 24.10 Figured Bass and the Chromatic Step-Descent Bass

Realize in four voices and analyze.

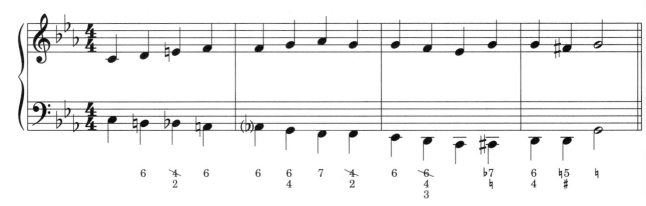

EXERCISE 24.11 Differentiation of Diatonic and Mixture Progressions

Below are diatonic progressions in major keys that are represented by roman numerals. Determine whether the roman numerals correctly represent what you hear, or whether mixture has been invoked. If what is played is what is written, write "OK." If the progressions contain mixture, then amend roman numerals and figured bass to reflect the chromaticism. For example, given the notated progression I–vi–ii$_6$–V–I, but you hear mixture on both the vi and the ii harmony, then you would write "♭VI" and "ii°$_6$."

A. I–ii°$_6$–V$_7$–I

B. I–vii°$_6$–I$_6$–IV–V

C. I–V–vi–ii$_6$–V–I

D. I–vi–IV–V–I

E. I–iii–iv–V–vi

F. I–V$_6$–IV$_6$–V–vi

EXERCISE 24.12 Dictation

Notate bass and soprano of each progression. Expect one or two examples of modal mixture in each progression. Analyze.

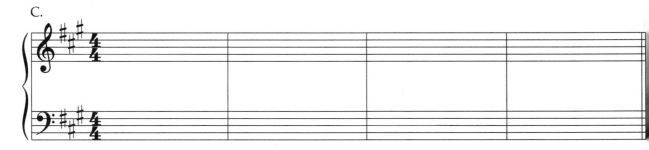

D. 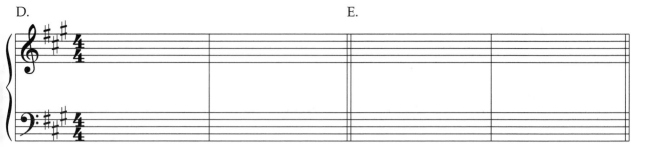 E.

F.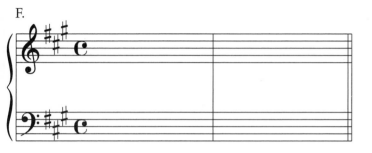

G.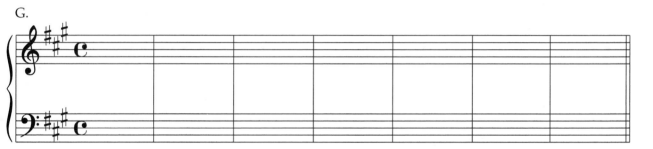

EXERCISE 24.13 Keyboard: Plagal Relations and Other Types of Mixture

Play progressions A, B, and C in major keys up to and including two sharps and flats; play progression D in minor keys up to two sharps and flats. Be able to sing the bass while playing the other voices.

A. I–iv–ii°$^4_3$–I   C. I–VI–IV♮–♭–V7–♭VI

B. I–iii–IV–iv–I   D. i–V$_6$–V$^4_3$ of IV–IV$_6$–iv$_6$–V

EXERCISE 24.14 Analysis and Dictation of Plagal Relations and Other Chromatic Chords

Notate the bass and provide a roman numeral analysis.

A.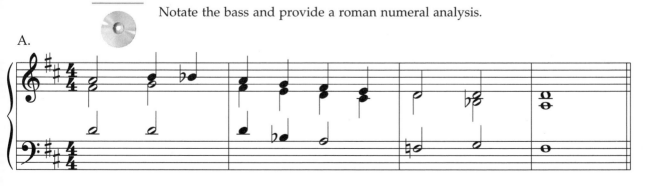

B.

C.   Chopin, Mazurka in B♭ major, op. 17, no. 1, BI 77

EXERCISE 24.15   Analysis of III♯ and VI♯ in Major

Provide roman numerals for the progressions that incorporate III♯ and VI♯. Be aware that III and VI are often only apparent mixture harmonies (that is, they may simply be applied chords to vi and ii, respectively).

A.   Beethoven, *Presto*, Piano Trio No. 5 in D major, "Ghost," op. 70, no. 1

B. Beethoven, *Scherzo and Trio: Allegro,* Violin Sonata No. 5 in F major, "Spring," op. 24

What is unusual about the mixture harmony's function in the large-scale tonal framework?

C. This example modulates; label pivot.

D. Schubert, "Die Allmacht" ("Omnipotence"), op. 79, no. 2, D. 852

Gross ist Jehova, der Herr! Denn Himmel

Und Erde verkünden seine Macht.

Great is Jehova, the Lord! For heaven

And earth proclaim his might.

E. Chopin, *Poco più lento*, Nocturne in C minor, op. 48, no. 1, BI 142

EXERCISE 24.16   Melody Harmonization

Harmonize the following melody in G major; add as many mixture harmonies as possible. Your choices are: ii$^{\phi 6}_{5}$, ♭III, III♯, iv, ♭VI, and VI♯. Try playing your solution on the piano.

EXERCISE 24.17 Writing Plagal Relations, III(♯) and VI(♯)

Write the following progressions:
A. In E♭ major: I–III(♯)–IV–V7–♭VI
B. In B♭ major: I–VI(♯)–IV–V–I
C. In F major: I–♭VI–ii$^{ø6}_{5}$–V$^{4}_{2}$–I$_6$–III(♯)–IV–iv–I
D. In C major: V–V/♭VI–♭VI–iv♭–V/♭III–♭III–ii$^{ø6}_{5}$–I

EXERCISE 24.18 Figured Bass Incorporating Plagal Relations, III(♯) and VI(♯)

Realize the figured bass below in four voices. Analyze.

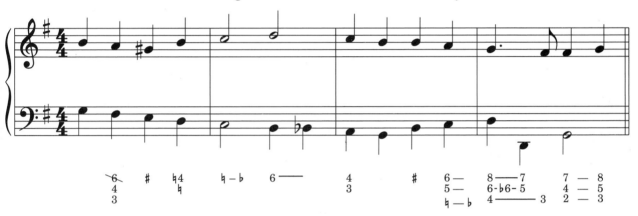

EXERCISE 24.19 Keyboard: Potpourri of Mixture Progressions

Play the following mixture progressions that include step-descent bass, plagal relations and other mixture chords as written, and in major keys up to and including two sharps and flats.

A.

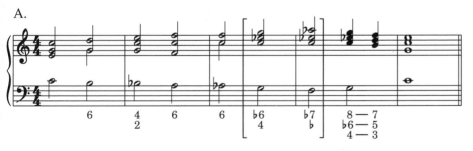

B.

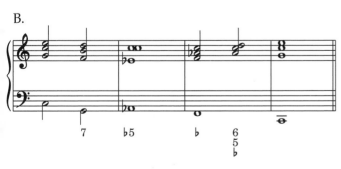

C.

EXERCISE 24.20   Illustrations

Complete the following tasks in four voices. Analyze.

A.   Modulate from D major to its dominant. Cast the progression as a two-phrase progressive period. Include a suspension and an example of mixture in both the original key and the dominant key.

B.   Modulate from F major to its diatonic submediant. Include a proper use of ♭III in the original key and a step-descent bass in the new key.

C.   Modulate from C minor to its VI. Include at least two applied chords in the original key and two suspensions and an example of mixture in the new key.

EXERCISE 24.21   Composition

Write a sixteen-measure double period that fleshes out the model below. Choose a meter and melodic structure (parallel or contrasting). Begin in G major and move to its V. Details of each phrase follow.

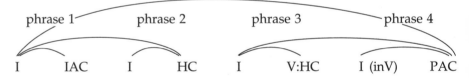

Phrase 1: Include a sequence of your choice that uses suspensions.
Phrase 2: Include one applied chord and one example of mixture.
Phrase 3: Use a mixture harmony as the pivot leading to the HC in V.
Phrase 4: Include a step-descent bass.

EXERCISE 24.22   Keyboard: Recipes

Below are two sets of ingredients for making two satisfying main-course progressions that incorporate mixture. Unfortunately, they appear in a jumbled order; you will need to place them in a logical order before combining them into a finished product.

Recipe 1:

one PAC with suspension
slowly spread one step-descent bass
place in the key of D major
a dash of ♭III
tonicize any closely related key
a measure or two of an A2 (D3/A4) sequence

mix the above ingredients in $\frac{4}{4}$ meter
This batch will fit in a six- to ten-measure baking pan.

Recipe 2:

one teaspoon of $\flat$VI
prolong tonic with a bass arpeggiation
sprinkle in two suspensions
close with a tonicization of III
begin in C minor
knead in one passing $\frac{6}{4}$ chord
gently add one D2 (D5/A4) sequence
place in an eight-measure triple-meter ovenproof container

CHAPTER 25

Expansion of Modal Mixture Harmonies: Chromatic Tonicization and Modulation

EXERCISE 25.1   Analysis

Listen to the following examples of prepared (i.e., pivot chord(s) chromatic tonicizations. Then do the following:

1. Locate and label the chromatic tonicization.
2. Locate and interpret the pivot chord or pivot area.
3. Indicate the large-scale harmonic function of the chromatic tonicization via a mini-form diagram that places the structural harmonies of the excerpt within one fluid harmonic motion.

Example A has been done for you.

A. Beethoven, *Adagio molto expressivo*, Violin Sonata, op. 24, "Spring"

B.   Beethoven, *Largo appassionato*, Piano Sonata No. 2 in A major, op. 2, no. 2

C. Mozart, *Allegro*, String Quartet in A major, K. 464
Bracket and label the formal construction that occurs in mm. 1–16.

augmented 6th
chord as pre-dominant

EXERCISE 25.2   Figured Bass

Each of the figured basses below contains a chromatic tonicization. Realize in four voices and analyze; mark the pivot.

EXERCISE 25.3   Melody Harmonization

Harmonize the soprano melodic fragments below in four voices, each of which implies a chromatic tonicization. Analyze with roman numerals and mark the pivot carefully.

(Continued)

E.

EXERCISE 25.4   Multiple Harmonizations of a Soprano Melody

Below is a modulating soprano melody that may be harmonized in a variety of ways. On a separate sheet of manuscript paper, find at least two different solutions, analyze, and then harmonize one of your solutions in four voices.

EXERCISE 25.5   Keyboard: Figured Bass

Realize in four voices the following figured bass that modulates to a chromatic third-related key. Analyze.

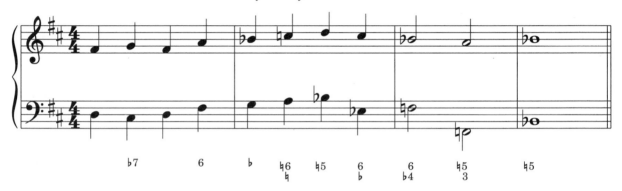

EXERCISE 25.6   Analysis and Dictation

Below are two score examples, each of which modulates. The bass lines, however, are partially or completely missing.

1. Listen to each example, then notate the bass.
2. Provide roman numerals, circling any pivots. Watch carefully for motions to the following keys:

in major keys: ♭III, iii, V, ♭VI, vi
in minor keys: III, v, VI

A.

(Continued)

(*Continued*)

EXERCISE 25.7   Notation of Chromatic Modulations

The following examples modulate either to ♭III or ♭VI. The first three are short; the next two are slightly longer. On a separate sheet of manuscript paper, notate the bass and soprano; provide roman numerals. Remember, the standard modulatory technique establishes the initial key, employs a pivot (using a mixture chord as a pre-dominant), establishes the new key, and closes with a PAC. A and B have two sharps, C and D have one sharp, and E has two sharps.

EXERCISE 25.8   Keyboard: Soprano Harmonization

Harmonize the soprano fragments below, each of which implies a chromatic modulation. The destinations include: ♭VI, ♭III, VI♯, and III♯

EXERCISE 25.9 Analysis of Prepared and Common-Tone Chromatic Modulations

Below are two types of chromatic-third modulations: pivot chord and common tone.

1. Label the chromatic destination using roman numerals.
2. Determine whether the composer has used a pivot chord modulation (in which a mixture chord in the first key becomes a diatonic chord in the new key), or a common-tone modulation (a single pitch is reinterpreted in the new key). If you encounter a pivot chord modulation, mark the pivot. If you encounter a common-tone modulation, circle and beam the common pitch class(es).

A. Brahms, "Die Mainacht"

(Continued)

Ü - ber - hül - let vom Laub   gir - ret ein Tau - ben - paar

B.   Chopin, Mazurka in A♭ major, op. 17, no. 3

C.   Chopin, Etude in A♭ major, op. 10, no. 10

D. Brahms, #4, from Vier ernste Gesänge ("Four Serious Songs"), for Bass and Piano, op. 121

EXERCISE 25.10   Analysis and Dictation

The examples below from the literature include prepared and unprepared chromatic modulations. Identify pivots when appropriate. For some, a considerable amount of score is given; for others, only a few bass notes, or perhaps only a staff, is given. Notate bass lines and provide roman numerals.

A. Beethoven, "Dimmi, ben mio" ("Hoffnung"), *Vier Arietten*, op. 82, no. 1

(Continued)

(*Continued*)

... E non invidio ai Dei
La lor' divinità!
Con un tuo sguardo solo,
Cara, con un sorriso
Tu m'apri il paradiso
Di mia felicità!

Dimmi, ben mio, che m'ami,
Dimmi che mia tu sei.

... Und schnell in ihrer Hand
Wird Leid in Glück gewandt.
Kühn nur zum Ziele streben,
Treu nur der Hoffnung leben!
Und aus den Stürmen
Bricht der Gewährung süsses Licht.

Nimmer dem liebenden Herzen
Zürnen auf ewig die Götter;

B. Mozart, *Andante,* String Quartet No. 9 in C major, K. 169

(Continued)

(*Continued*)

C.   Wagner, *Das Rheingold*, scene 2

(Continued)

(*Continued*)

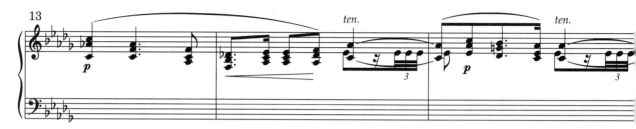

EXERCISE 25.11   Harmonizing Soprano Fragments

Harmonize the following soprano fragments and complete any required tasks.
Then, provide roman numerals, work out a good bass line, and add inner voices.

A.

Include the following:

1. tonicization
2. diminished seventh chord

B.

Include the following:

1. at least one example of tonicization
2. one example of mixture

C.

Include the following:

1. a sequence
2. an applied °7 chord
3. a modulation (close in new tonal area)

EXERCISE 25.12 Writing Common-Tone and Other Types of Modulations

Complete the following tasks in four voices; analyze.

A. Modulate from C major to A♭ major using a common-tone modulation. Include a D2 (D5/A4) sequence in C major.

B. Modulate from E major to ♭III using a common-tone modulation.

C. Modulate from D minor to B♭ major using a common-chord modulation. Include a D3 (D4/A2) sequence in D minor.

D. Modulate from B♭ major to D major using a mixture chord pivot.

E. Modulate from A major to F major using any sequence as a pivot.

F. Modulate from G major to B♭ major using any sequence as a pivot.

G. Given an F minor triad as a pivot, modulate from:

   1. C major to A♭ major.
   2. E♭ major to C minor.
   3. A♭ major to F minor.

H. Given a G major triad as a pivot, modulate from:

   1. C major to E minor.
   2. E♭ major to G major.
   3. B major to E major.
   4. B♭ major to E♭ major.

EXERCISE 25.13 Keyboard: Illustrations

Complete the following tasks in four voices.

A. Given the key of D major, use iv as a pivot to tonicize ♭III.

B. Given the key of D major, use iv as a pivot to tonicize ♭VI.

C. Given the key of C major, use ♭VI as a pivot to tonicize ♭III.

D. Modulate from G major to ♭III. Include two suspensions and a sequence.

EXERCISE 25.14 Keyboard: Pitch Reinterpretation

Follow the instructions below to construct chromatic tonicizations. Each progression should contain approximately twelve chords.

A. Modulate from D major to B♭; use $\hat{1}$ in the original key as the common-note pivot. Include one voice exchange and two $^6_4$ chords.

B. Modulate from F major to A♭; use $\hat{5}$ in the original key as the common-note pivot. Include one voice exchange and one nondominant seventh chord.

C. Modulate from G major to E♭ major; use a common-chord pivot (it must be a mixture chord in the first key). Begin with an ECM (embedded cadential motion) and include two suspensions within the progression.

D. Modulate from C major to E major; use a common-chord pivot (it must be a mixture chord in the first key). Include a step-descent bass.

E. Modulate from F major to A major; use $\hat{3}$ in the original key as the common-note pivot. Include an example of modal mixture in each key.

EXERCISE 25.15   Interactive Analysis

Schubert, "An Emma" ("To Emma"), D. 311c

ach, du lebst im_ Licht, du lebst im_ Licht! mei - ner Lie - be lebst du nicht,   mei - ner Lie - be lebst du

nich.   Kann der Lie - be süss' Ver-lan - gen,   Em-ma, kann's ver-gäng - lich sein?

Was da-hin ist und ver-gan - gen,   Em-ma, kann's die Lie - be sein? Ih - rer

Flam - me Him - mels-gluth,   stirbt sie wie ein ir - disch Gut?

This song presents chromatic-third relations prepared by modal mixture. Study the text and listen to the song. Then, analyze to the best of your ability, using roman numerals. Star any passages whose resolutions or progressions you find puzzling or interesting. Then, attempt a second analysis with the following leading discussion guiding you.

Weit in nebelgrauer Ferne
Liegt mir das vergangne Glück,
Nur an einem schönen Sterne
Weilt mit Liebe noch der Blick.
Aber, wie des Sternes Pracht,
Ist es nur ein Schein der Nacht.

Far in the great misty distance
lies my past happiness.
My gaze still lingers fondly
on one lovely star alone;
but the splendor of the star,
it is only an illusion of the night.

Deckte dir der lange Schlummer,   If the long sleep of night
Dir der Tod die Augen zu,   had closed your eyes
Dich besässe doch mein Kummer,   my grief might still possess you;
Meinem Herzen lebtest du.   you would live on in my heart.
Aber ach! du lebst im Licht,   But oh, you live in the light,
Meiner Liebe lebst du nicht.   but you do not live for my love

Kann der Liebe süss Verlangen,   Emma, can love's sweetness
Emma, kann's vergänglich sein?   fade and die?
Was dahin ist und vergangen,   That which is past and gone,
Emma, kann's die Liebe sein?   Emma—can that be love?
Ihrer Flamme Himmelsglut,   Can the heavenly glow of its ardor die,
Stirbt sie wie ein irdisch Gut?   like some earthly possession?

(trans. John Reed *The Schubert Song Companion*)

The goal of *Lied* analysis is to figure out how the musical relations you find may be aligned with the underlying poetic drama. The subject of this poem is timeless. A jilted lover reflecting on happier times is jarred back repeatedly to the reality of his loss. The rhyme scheme of the text is ababcc. The last two lines of each strophe are segregated both by rhyme scheme and meaning, acting as a refrain. Within the first two strophes this refrain and the preceding verse are set in opposition to one another. The verse expresses the protagonist's longing for love while the refrain redirects this thought toward the painful truth. The first verse emphasizes past happiness, and the distance between the speaker and the object of his gaze, the star, is symbolic of the time that separates him from Emma, the object of his affection.

1. Are particular words highlighted in the musical setting? By what means? Consider the use of accidentals, chromatic harmony, and dramatic pause.
2. Locate all the A major triads. Are certain words associated with this chord and with D minor (its resolution chord)?
3. Are there harmonic progressions left incomplete? How might these interact with the text?
4. In the second verse (mm. 20ff.), consider the analogy of death with night and slumber. Is the beloved dead, or only dead to the love of the speaker? Is there a change in the speaker's perspective? Where is the climax in this section?
5. In the closing verse, the speaker poses a question to his beloved: If true love can never die, and that which we shared has, then how could it have been love? Why is there the curious sojourn into A♭ major?

EXERCISE 25.16   Comparative Analysis

Analyze the excerpts below from Beethoven's and Schubert's settings of Goethe's poem "Kennst du das Land?" Focus on chromaticism that results from tonicization and modal mixture. Then, study the two text settings, and compare and contrast the way Beethoven and Schubert have merged text and music.

A.   Beethoven, "Mignon," op. 75, no. 1

Ziemlich langsam

Kennst   du   das Land,   wo   die   Ci - tro - nen   blüh'n, ___   im

B.   Schubert, "Kennst du das Land?" ("Mignons Gesang") ("Do You Know the Land?"), D. 321

(Continued)

(*Continued*)

K ennst du das Land, wo die Zitronen blühn,	Do you know where the lemon grows,
Im dunkeln Laub die Gold-Orangen glühn,	In dark foliage the golden-orange glows,
Ein sanfter Wind vom blauen Himmel weht,	A gentle breeze blows from the blue sky,
Die Myrte still und hoch der Lorbeer steht?	Do the myrtle and the laurel, stand high?
Kennst du es wohl? . . .	Do you know it well? . . .
Kennst du das Haus? Auf Säulen ruht sein Dach.	Do you know the the house, its roof on columns fine?
Es glänzt der Saal, es schimmert das Gemach,	Its hall glows brightly and its chambers shine,
Und Marmorbilder stehn und sehn mich an:	And marble figures stand and gaze at me:

Was hat man dir, du armes Kind, getan?	What have they done, oh poor child, to you?
Kennst du es wohl? . . .	Do you know it well? . . .

EXERCISE 25.17   Keyboard: Unfigured Basses

Realize the following unfigured bass and soprano melody in four voices. Analyze. Sing either outer voice while playing the other voices.

CHAPTER 26

The Neapolitan Sixth Chord (♭II₆)

EXERCISE 26.1   ♭II Dictation

On a separate sheet of manuscript paper, notate the bass voice in the following short progressions (c. six chords). Include roman numerals. All examples are in $\frac{4}{4}$ and contain one sharp except for Example J, which has four sharps.

EXERCISE 26.2   Spelling, Identifying, and Writing ♭II₆

Given the following triads, determine the minor key in which each triad functions as ♭II₆ and provide a key signature. Then, resolve each as required. You will need to correct the two misspelled Neapolitan harmonies (only one of the members of the chord is misspelled).

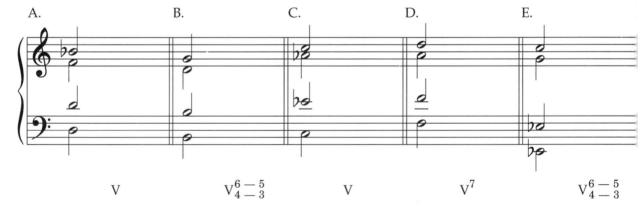

EXERCISE 26.3   More Spelling, Identifying, and Writing ♭II₆

Given is the bass of ♭II₆ chords in various keys. Determine the key for each example, and provide a key signature. Then, complete the ♭II₆ chord in four voices (double the bass in each case) and precede and follow it as required.

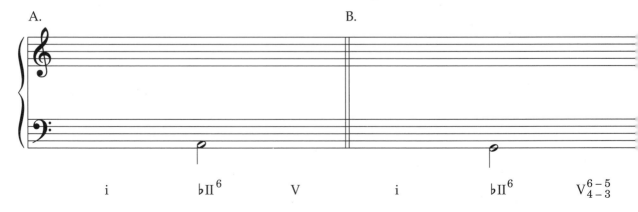

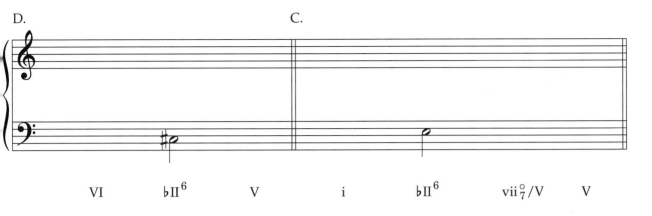

VI   ♭II⁶   V   i   ♭II⁶   vii°₇/V   V

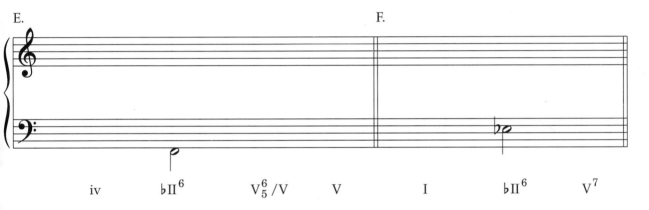

iv   ♭II⁶   V⁶₅/V   V   I   ♭II⁶   V⁷

EXERCISE 26.4   Figured Bass

Realize in four voices the following figured basses. All examples contain one flat.

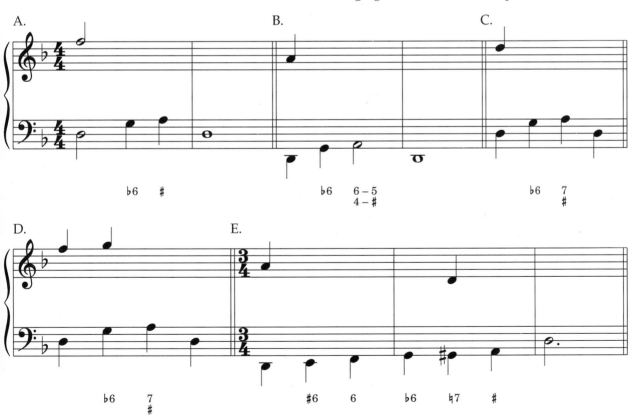

EXERCISE 26.5   Harmonic Progressions

Choose a suitable meter and rhythmic setting and write the following progressions in four voices. Analyze. Play your progressions on the piano in keyboard style. Be able to sing either outer voice while playing the remaining three voices.

A.   D minor: i–VI–♭II6–V–i   C.   C minor: i–V$_6$/III–III–♭II$_6$–cad. $^6_4$–$^5_3$–i

B.   B minor: i–vii°$_6$–i$_6$–♭II$_6$–vii°$_7$/V–V–I   D.   G major: I–iv–♭II$_6$–vii°$_7$/V–V–I

EXERCISE 26.6   Longer Figured Bass

Realize the figured bass and given melody below by adding inner voices. Analyze. What type of progression opens the exercise?

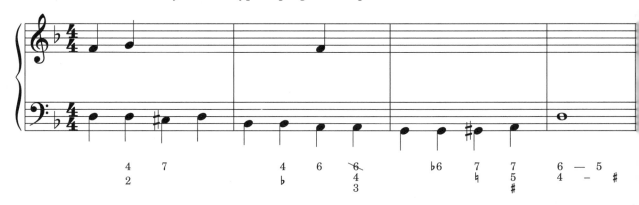

EXERCISE 26.7   Unfigured Bass and Melody

Based on the harmonic implications of the bass and soprano, add inner voices and analyze.

EXERCISE 26.8   Melodic Fragments

Write a logical bass line, analyze, and add inner voices.

A.

B.

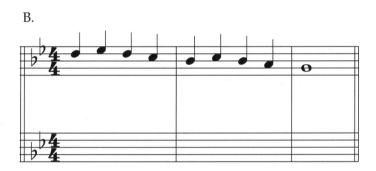

C.

EXERCISE 26.9　Bass Notation

Listen to and study each example, the upper voices for which are given. Notate the bass line and provide roman numerals for each. Arrows indicate where to notate bass notes.

A.　Schubert, "Am See" ("By the Lake"), D. 124

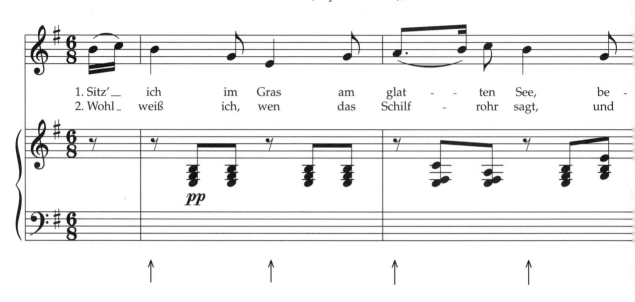

Sitz' ich im Gras am glatten

Beschleicht die Seele banges Weh,
mit Geisterarmen . . .

Wohl weiss ich, was das Schilfrohr
sagt,
und was das Lied des Vogels klagt,
ach Luft und Flut und . . .

See, If I sit in the grass by the smooth
lake,
an anxious woe steals upon my soul,
embraced by a spectre . . .

Well I know what the bulrush is saying,

and what song the bird laments:
ah, breeze and stream and . . .

B.　Chopin, Waltz in A minor, op. 34, no. 2, BI 64

C.   Schumann, "Hör' ich das Liedchen klingen" ("I Hear the Dear Song Sound-ing"), *Dichterliebe*, op. 48, no. 10
This example contains a tonicization of iv.

Hör' ich das Liedchen klingen,
Das einst die Liebste sang,
So will mir die Brust zerspringen
Von wildem Schmerzendrang.

I hear the dear song sounding
That my beloved once sang.
And my heart wants to burst so strongly
From the savage pressure of pain.

D.

E.

EXERCISE 26.10   Keyboard: Melody Harmonization

Harmonize the short soprano melodies in two different ways, one of which must include an example of ♭II. Hint: Both settings may not need to be in minor. Feel free to include applied harmonies and mixture. Analyze.

EXERCISE 26.11   Notation of Phrases Incorporating the Neapolitan (I)

Determine whether the progression you hear contains a single harmonic motion or whether it is divided into two or more subphrases. If it is divided, determine each subphrase's function (e.g., to prolong tonic). Analyze with roman numerals; bracket and label sequences. Then, listen again and sing the bass, and notate it. You may encounter a modulation to a closely related key.

A.

B.

C.

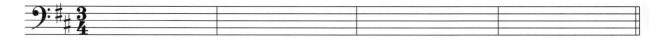

D.

E.

F.

G.

EXERCISE 26.12   Notation of Progressions Incorporating the Neapolitan (II)

Provide roman numerals and notate both bass and soprano for Examples A–H, each of which is four measures. Example I, from the literature, occupies eight measures. Notate only the bass and analyze.

A.

B.

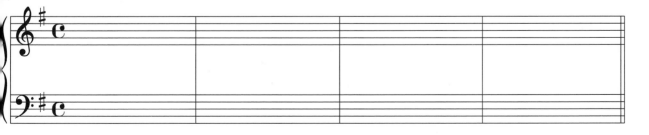

C.

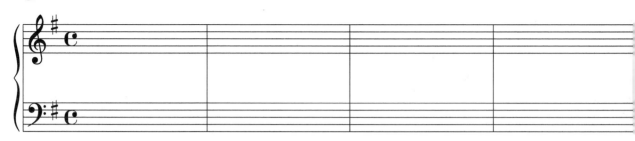

D.

E.

F.

G.

H.

I. Vivaldi, Concerto in C major for Two Violins, F.XI/44, Ry 114, P27, Ri 493

EXERCISE 26.13   Illustrations

Determine a logical ordering of the musical elements below, then incorporate them into a progression in four voices. Analyze your work. Note: You might be able to combine two or more steps.

A. In the key of C minor, write a progression in $\frac{4}{4}$ that

1. tonicizes the minor dominant.
2. includes an example of ♭II₆ in the tonic and the dominant areas.
3. includes two suspensions.
4. includes a step-descent bass.
5. includes an applied chord.

B. In the key of E minor, write a progression in $\frac{6}{8}$ that

1. tonicizes III.
2. includes a neighbor motive; it should occur in various contexts, either harmonized or unharmonized as a nonharmonic tone.
3. includes an example of mixture in the new key.
4. includes a sequence of your choice in either key.
5. includes an example of ♭II₆ in the first key.

EXERCISE 26.14 Keyboard: Figured Bass

Realize in four voices and analyze the figured bass below using two levels.

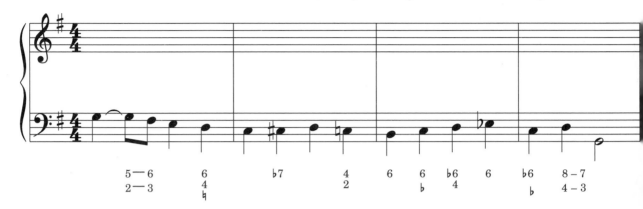

EXERCISE 26.15 The Expanded Neapolitan in Homophonic Settings

 Provide roman numerals and a bass line for the following examples.

A.

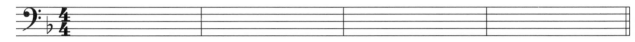

B.

C.

D.

EXERCISE 26.16 The Expanded Neapolitan in Figuration

Notate the bass voice and provide roman numerals for the following figurated examples of expanded Neapolitans; the last two are taken from the literature.

A.

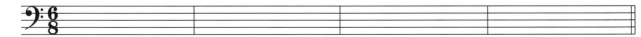

B.

C.

D.

E.   Schubert, *Trio*, Violin Sonata in A minor, op. posth. 137, no. 2, D. 385

EXERCISE 26.17   Keyboard: Illustrations

Complete the illustrations in the order that is described below.

A.   In D minor: expand tonic, include $\flat$II$_6$, lead to V with an applied °7 chord; close with an HC

B.   In A minor: a D2 (D5/A4) sequence with alternating nondominant sevenths that leads to $\flat$II$_6$; close with a PAC

C.   In F major: expand tonic using a descending bass arpeggiation; tonicize iii using a $\flat$II$_6$ in that key; close with a PAC in the key of iii

D.   In C major: establish tonic; tonicize $\flat$III; move to cadential $^6_4$ chord, close with a PAC

E.   In G minor: establish tonic; tonicize III; include an A2 (D3/A4) sequence with applied chords that leads to VI; use $\flat$II$_6$ as the pre-dominant; lead to V with a vii°$_7$/V and close with a PAC

F.   In D major: establish tonic; tonicize $\flat$VI; continue a descending arpeggiation to $\flat$II; close with a PAC in D major

EXERCISE 26.18 Keyboard: Figured Bass

Realize the figured bass in four voices; analyze using two levels. Not all suspensions may be able to be prepared. You may write in seven or eight soprano pitches.

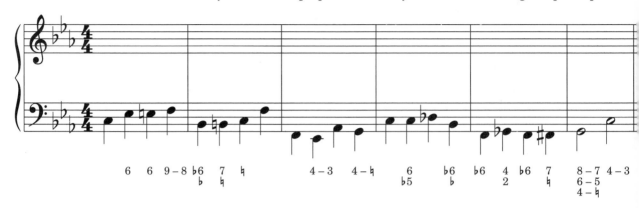

EXERCISE 26.19 Longer Analytical Projects

A. Locatelli, *Largo*, Sonata No. 3 in G minor, *Twelve Sonatas for Flute and Continuo*

1. What is the form of this piece?
2. The interval of the third, especially encompassing $\hat{1}$–$\hat{3}$, is very important throughout the piece. Mark various statements of the third. Explore how thirds in multiple voices may occur simultaneously, creating voice exchanges and other interesting contrapuntal motions.
3. A progressive period occurs in the A section. Analyze the pivot area. Compare this pivot with that which leads back to the tonic at the end of the digression.
4. Label all sequences.
5. Perform a roman numeral analysis of mm. 1–4.

B.   Brahms, Waltz in E major, op. 39, no. 12

1. What is the form of this piece?
2. What is the overall tonal motion in the first part?
3. a. What important harmonic change occurs in m. 13ff.
   b. Why do you think Brahms employs this harmonic technique? (Hint: Where does it go?)
4. What harmony is expanded in mm. 16–20? What is unusual about the expansion? (Hint: What makes it unstable and why would Brahms have written it this way?)

EXERCISE 26.20   Potpourri of Activities

Complete the tasks below in four voices. Be aware of expansions of ♭II. Analyze.

A.   Unfigured bass with soprano

B.   Figured bass with soprano

EXERCISE 26.21   Road Map

In D minor, complete the tasks below

A.   Establish tonic using any contrapuntal progression that includes a suspension.

B.   Tonicize III; include a mixture chord within the tonicization.

C.   Using an A2 (D3/A4) sequence with applied chords, move to VI (of D minor) and briefly tonicize that harmony.

D.   Tonicize ♭II using at least four chords.

E.   Using ♭II as a pivot, reinterpret it in the key of iv (of D minor) and close using a PAC in the new key of iv. Include ♭II in the closing progression and at least two suspensions.

Optional: Orchestrate your progression for string quartet or piano and voice (in which case you must design an accompanimental texture).

EXERCISE 26.22   Soprano Harmonization

Harmonize in four voices the following soprano melodies. Look for opportunities to incorporate the Neapolitan, mixture harmonies, and sequences. Analyze. Be able to play your progressions on the piano.

A.

B.

C.

EXERCISE 26.23   Dictation of Phrase-Model Expansions

Given the tonal model: i–$\flat$II–V–i. Each model is followed by a series of variations and expansions that flesh out its basic harmonic progression components with additional harmonies that occupy from two to four measures. Notate the outer voices and analyze each of the expansions.

Phrase model 1.

b: $\natural$6 $\sharp$

Expansion 1.   2.

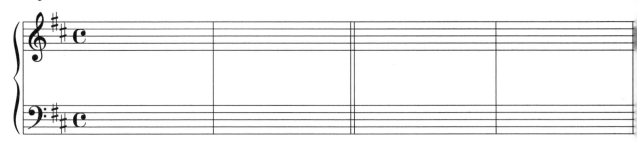

            b:
3.

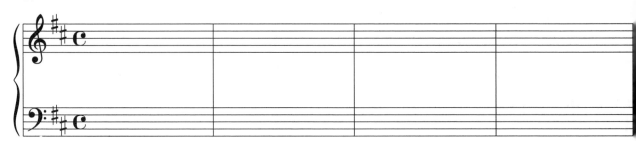

4.

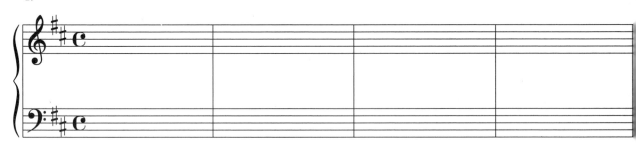

Phrase model 2.

Expansion 1.   2.

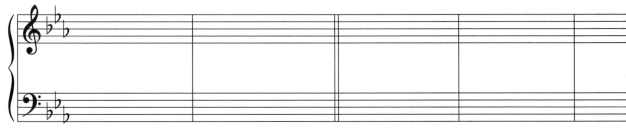

3.

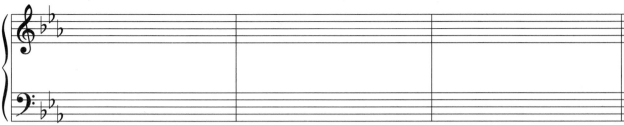

4.

5.

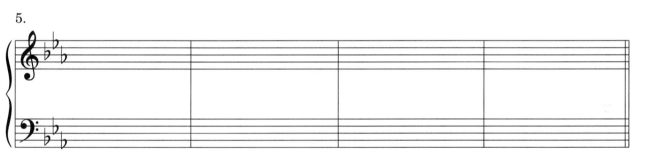

6.

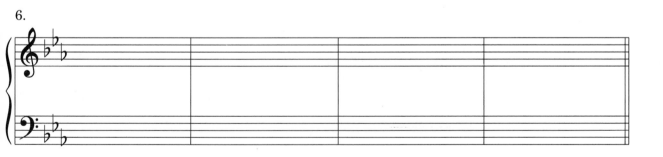

CHAPTER 27

The Augmented Sixth Chord

EXERCISE 27.1   Listening and Analysis

Listen to and analyze each of the following examples. If you encounter a +6 chord, label its type: "It. $\frac{6}{3}$," "Ger. $\frac{6}{5}$," or "Fr. $\frac{4}{3}$."

A.   Bach, "Ich hab' mein' Sach' Gott heimgestellt," BWV 351

1.   The pitch that creates the characteristic interval of the augmented sixth appears just after the other chord tones of the sonority; how does Bach postpone this pitch?
2.   Convert the ii°$_6$ chord in m. 2 into a ♭II$_6$ (Neapolitan) harmony.

B.   Mozart, *Allegretto,* Piano Trio No. 7 in E♭ major, K. 498

C.   Beethoven, *Finale: Allegro,* Violin Sonata No. 7 in C Minor, op. 30, no. 2
One could argue that all three forms (a world tour) of the augmented sixth appear in this example. Label each form.

Allegro

D. Mozart, *Allegro*, Piano Concerto in E♭ major, K. 449
Include a phrase/period diagram.

(Continued)

(*Continued*)

E.   Schubert, Waltz in F major, *36 Originatänze*, D. 365, no. 34

1.   The dominant harmony in m. 3 might be viewed as a ninth chord since the D^5, (a ninth above the bass) is not treated as a dissonance (i.e., it is not a passing or neighboring tone or a suspension). Yet one can also view the ninth as resolving in m. 5, making it only an apparent chord tone. Which interpretation do you prefer?

2.   What is the form of this piece? (Hint: Is this a binary form or merely a period?)

F.   Mozart, *Allegro,* String Quartet No. 15 in D minor, K. 421

1.   What type of bass line occurs twice in this example? What is the basic difference between the two appearances?

2.   How would you explain the dissonant B♭ in violin I of m. 3?

3.   How does Mozart prepare in the first phrase the augmented sixth chord that appears in the second phrase?

EXERCISE 27.2 Spelling Augmented Sixth Chords

Notate the following augmented sixth chords and resolve them to the dominant. Add necessary chromaticism rather than use key signatures.

C minor:	G minor:	D major:	A major:	C♯ minor:	B minor:
Ger $\frac{6}{5}$	Fr $\frac{4}{3}$	It 6	It 6	Fr $\frac{4}{3}$	Ger $\frac{6}{5}$

C.

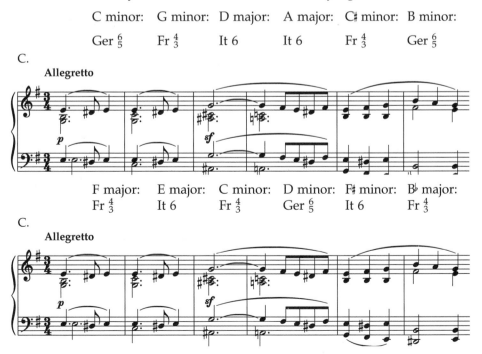

F major:	E major:	C minor:	D minor:	F♯ minor:	B♭ major:
Fr $\frac{4}{3}$	It 6	Fr $\frac{4}{3}$	Ger $\frac{6}{5}$	It 6	Fr $\frac{4}{3}$

C.

EXERCISE 27.3   Identification of Augmented Sixth Chords

Listen to the examples below and label pre-dominant type; your choices are: iv, ii°$_6$, ♭II$_6$, or +6 (specify type of +6; remember that the It. $^6_3$ moves directly to V and the Ger $^6_5$ moves to a cad. $^6_4$).

A. ___ B.___ C. ___ D. ___ E. ___ F. ___ G. ___ H. ___
I. ___ J. ___ K. ___ L. ___ M. ___ N. ___ O. ___

EXERCISE 27.4   Bass Line Notation of Augmented Sixth Chords

Notate the bass and analyze the following examples with pre-dominant harmonies that include the augmented sixth chord. Focus first on the underlying chord progression and the type of pre-dominant. One way to distinguish supertonic harmonies (including ♭II) from augmented sixth harmonies is that the bass of supertonic harmonies ascends to V but the bass of the augmented sixth descends to V. Thus, once you determine the bass's motion, you need only distinguish between ii and ♭II.

A.

B.

C.

D.

E.

F.

G.

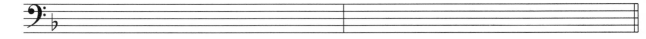

H.

I.

J.

EXERCISE 27.5   Longer Dictation

 Notate the bass and soprano of the four-measure examples and analyze. Examples C and D modulate.

A.

B.

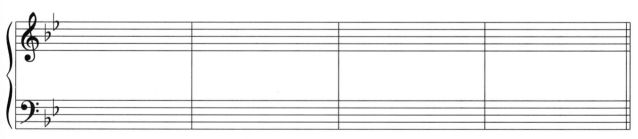

C.

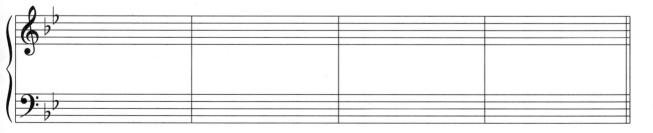

D.

EXERCISE 27.6   Dictation of Figurated Examples

Notate the bass lines of each of the four-measure phrases and analyze with roman numerals.

A.

B.

C.

D.   Haydn, *Adagio non lento,* String Quartet in B♭ major, op. 50, no. 1, Hob. III. 44

E.   Gluck, Sorrowing Mortal, from *Orpheus,* act. I, no. 23

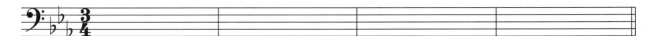

EXERCISE 27.7   Motion to and from Augmented Sixth Chords

Determine and label the key in which each of the augmented sixth chords below occurs. Then resolve each chord to the dominant as shown in the first example. Follow these guidelines:

1.   Resolve the interval of the augmented sixth by expanding it such that each voice leads to an octave on $\hat{5}$.

2. Move the other two voices to the nearest chord tone of the dominant. Don't forget that the German sixth resolves to the cadential $^6_4$ (V^{6-5}_{4-3}).

3. Precede each +6 chord with a tonic harmony. Keep common tones when possible.

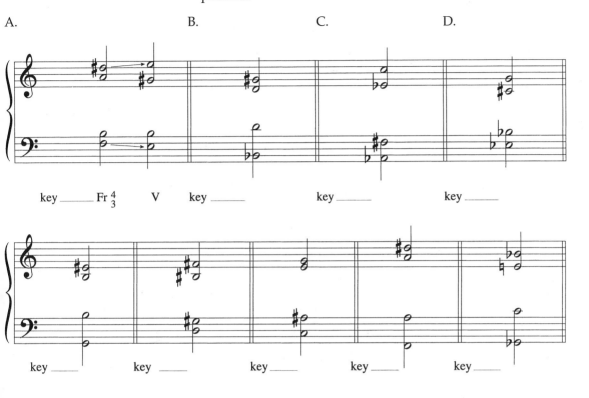

EXERCISE 27.8   Figured Basses

Realize the figured bases below in four voices and analyze.

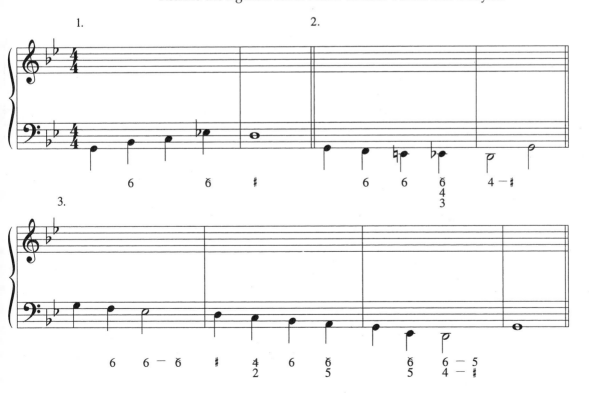

EXERCISE 27.9   Dictation and Analysis

The following excerpts include the upper voices. Notate the basses and include roman numerals.

A.   Schubert, "Wehmut" ("Melancholy"), op. 22, no. 2, D. 772

Langsam (Lento)

Wenn ich durch Wald und Fluren geh'

B.   Lamento di Magdellena

C.   Haydn, *Allegretto,* String Quartet in E♭ major, op. 76, no. 6, Hob. III. 80

D.   Beethoven, *Allegro con brio*, Piano Trio No. 3 in C minor, op. 1, no. 3

E.   Schubert, "Die Liebe hat gelogen" ("Love Has Lied"), op. 23, no. 1, D. 751

Die Liebe hat gelogen,   Love has lied,
Die Sorge lastet schwer,   Worries burden me heavily;

F.   Gluck, Sweet Affection, Heavenly Treasure, Trio, from *Orpheus*, act. III, no. 50

(Continued)

(*Continued*)

EXERCISE 27.10   Short Illustrations

On a separate sheet of manuscript paper, complete the following tasks in four voices. Analyze.

A. In G minor, write: i–It 6–V–i.

B. In B minor, write: i–Fr $\frac{4}{3}$–V$_7$–i.

C. In D minor, write the following progression: i–Ger $\frac{6}{5}$–cad. $\frac{6-5}{4-3}$–i.

D. In C minor, write: i–iv$_6$–Ger $\frac{6}{5}$–cad. $\frac{6-5}{4-3}$–i.

E. In A minor, harmonize the following soprano melody using any augmented sixth chord: $\hat{3}$–$\hat{4}$–$\sharp\hat{4}$–$\hat{5}$.

F. In E minor, write a progression that expands tonic, includes a Fr$\frac{4}{3}$, and closes with an HC.

G. In D minor, harmonize the following bass line; include any augmented sixth chord: $\hat{1}$–($\flat\hat{7}$)–$\hat{6}$–$\hat{5}$.

H. In F major, write a progression that includes an It $\frac{6}{3}$ chord and a suspension.

I. In G minor, write : i–vii°$_6$–i$_6$–iv–Fr$\frac{4}{3}$–V–i.

J. In D major, write a parallel interrupted period that contains two different types of +6 chords.

EXERCISE 27.11   Keyboard: Warm-Up and Review

The unfigured bass and soprano below contain sequences, applied chords, modulations, mixture, and the Neapolitan. Play in four voices and analyze using two levels.

EXERCISE 27.12 Melody Harmonization and Augmented Sixths

Study the melodic fragments below and harmonize each in four voices according to any instructions. Analyze.

A. Include an It $^6_3$ and step-descent bass

B. Include a Ger $^6_5$ and an applied chord

C.   Include a Fr $\frac{4}{3}$ and deceptive cadence

D.   Include an applied chord and an augmented sixth chord.

EXERCISE 27.13   Dictation of Expanded ♭VI and Conversion to Augmented Sixth

 Notate the bass and soprano lines for each excerpt except the last one, where you need to notate only the bass (do not notate repeated pitches). Analyze.

A.

B.

C.

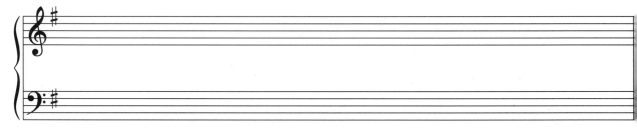

EXERCISE 27.14   Dictation of Modulations Featuring the
Augmented Sixth Chord

Each of the four modulating phrases contains a prominent augmented sixth chord. You are given the upper voices in the first two exercises; notate only the bass and analyze. Notate both soprano and bass for Examples C–D. Analyze using two levels.

A.

B.

C.

D.

EXERCISE 27.15 Figured Bass

Realize the figured bass below in four voices. Analyze.

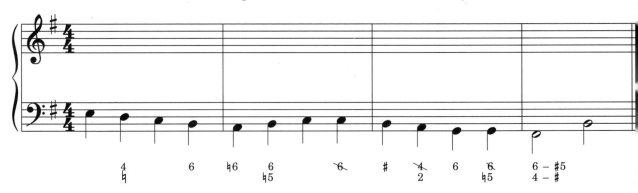

EXERCISE 27.16 Aural Examples from the Literature

Notate the bass for each of the examples below. Analyze.

A. Haydn, *Adagio*, Piano Sonata No. 38 in F major, Hob. XVI. 23

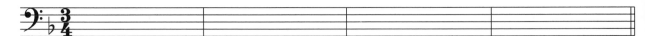

B. Haydn, *Adagio*, Piano Sonata in D major, Hob. XVI. 33

C. Beethoven, *Minore*, String Quartet No. 3 in D major, op. 18, no. 3

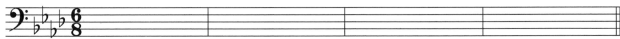

D. Schubert, Waltz in C minor, *Wiener Deutsche*, D. 128, no. 6.
This example is slightly longer (12 mm.), but the bass line should be easy to follow. What is the chromatic pre-dominant chord that leads to the final cadence?

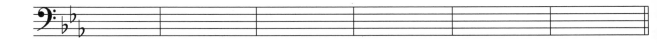

E.   Schumann, Waltz in A minor, *Albumblätter*, op. 124, no. 6

F.   Gluck, His Moving Elegies, from *Orpheus*, act II, no. 27
This example begins on V. What harmony is prolonged over this example?

EXERCISE 27.17   Illustrations

Complete the following tasks. Analyze.

A.   In D major, move to ♭VI, briefly prolong it through tonicization. Then, desta-bilize ♭VI by converting it into a Fr $\frac{4}{3}$. Close with a PAC.

B.   Write an eight-measure progressive period in A minor. In phrase one, estab-lish the key with any sequence that leads to the pre-dominant ♭II, and close with an HC. Close phrase two in any closely related key. Use an augmented sixth in the new key.

C.   Modulate from F major to ♭III. Use an augmented sixth chord in each key.

D.   Modulate from B minor to its VI. Use a chromatic step-descent bass in the original key. Employ any sequence in the new key and an augmented sixth chord.

EXERCISE 27.18   Analysis of Enharmonic Modulations Using the Augmented Sixth Chord

Identify the point at which the augmented sixth chord is transformed enhar-monically into a dominant in the following musical excerpts. Even though you will hear tonicizations, not real modulations, use the pivot chord labeling tech-nique. For example:

I: $\boxed{\text{Ger } \frac{6}{5}}$
♭II: $\boxed{\text{V}_7}$

Exercise C requires you to realize the given figured bass.

A.

B.

C.

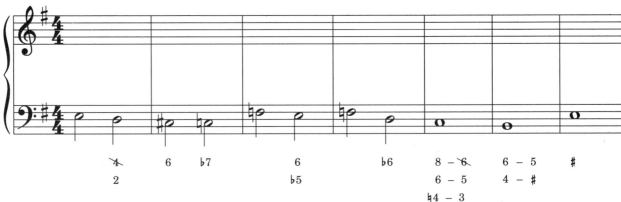

D. Beethoven, "Rage Over a Lost Penny," op. 129

E. Beethoven, *Nicht zu geschwind und sehr singbar vorzutragen,* Piano Sonata No. 27 in E major, op. 90, no. 2

F. Schubert, *Moderato,* Piano Sonata in A minor, op. 42, D. 845

G. Schubert, *Originaltänze,* op. 9, no. 14, D. 365

EXERCISE 27.19   Brainteaser

Consider the following two harmonies: C–E–G–B♭ and C–E–G–A♯. Determine the key in which these function as a dominant seventh and German sixth respectively. Then, write a progression that demonstrates each chord's behavior.

EXERCISE 27.20   Figured Bass

Realize the following figured bass; analyze.

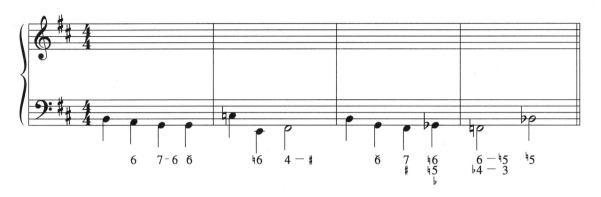

EXERCISE 27.21   Expanded Pre-Dominants and Augmented Sixth/Diminished Third Chords

Analyze the excerpts that combine extended pre-dominants and augmented sixth chords. Circle the pre-dominant area, then analyze each sonority.

A.   Haydn, *Allegretto,* Piano Sonata in E major, Hob. XVI. 31

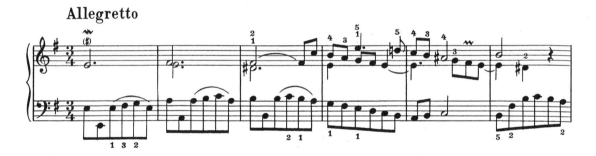

B.   Beethoven, *Larghetto espressivo,* String Quartet No. 11 in F minor, "Serioso," op. 95

C.   Gluck, Ritornello, from *Orpheus,* act I, no. 6

EXERCISE 27.22   Dictation

The following progressions contain expanded pre-dominants. Notate bass and soprano; analyze. Possible expansions are as follows:

- $iv \rightarrow P_4^6 \rightarrow iv_6$
- $iv_6 \rightarrow P_4^6 \rightarrow ii^{\circ}{}_6$
- $iv \rightarrow P_4^6 \rightarrow {+}6$

- $Ger\,{}_5^6 \rightarrow P_4^6 \rightarrow Ger\,{}^{\circ}3$
- $iv_6 \rightarrow P_4^6 \rightarrow {}^{\flat}II_6$

A.

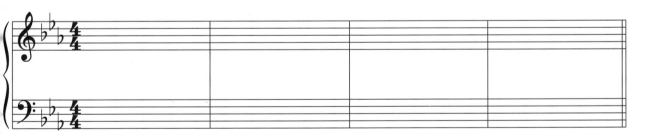

B.

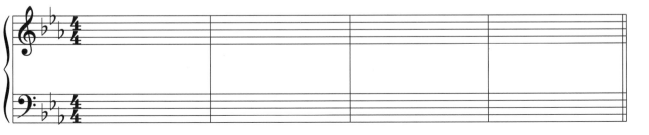

C.

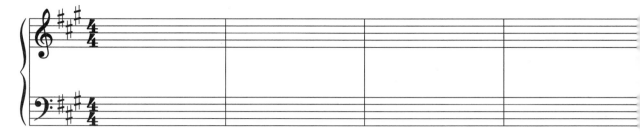

D.

EXERCISE 27.23   Writing the Diminished Third Chord

Write the following chords and resolve them to the dominant:

A.   Ger °3 in C minor
B.   Ger $\frac{6}{5}$ in D minor
C.   Ger °3 in C# minor

D.   Ger $\frac{6}{5}$—P$\frac{6}{4}$—Ger °3 in A minor
E.   Ger $\frac{6}{4}$—Ger °3 in G minor; include soprano voice exchange

EXERCISE 27.24   Figured and Unfigured Basses

Realize in four voices and analyze the figured and unfigured basses below.

EXERCISE 27.25   Writing

Complete the following passage in four-voice chorale style, given the following:

mm. 1–2: unfigured bass
mm. 3–4: melody harmonization
mm. 5–6: figured bass
mm. 7–8: figured bass + melody

Provide the remaining voices and analyze. Include one of each type of augmented sixth chord.

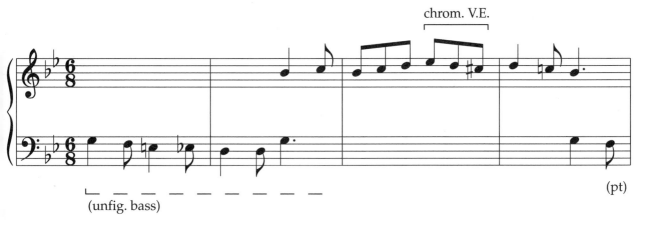

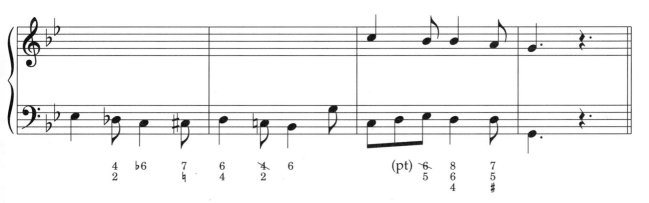

EXERCISE 27.26   Keyboard: Figured Bass

Add the inner voices to the following extended figured bass. Analyze using two levels. Be able to sing the bass while you play the other voices. You may write in one or two soprano pitches in each measure.

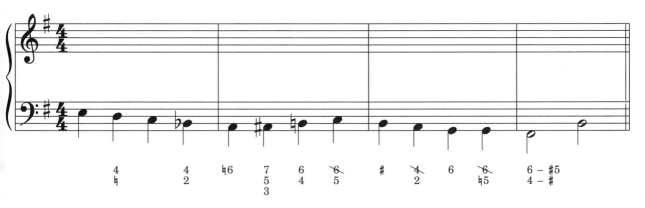

EXERCISE 27.27   Keyboard: Road Map

Below is a musical outline that includes instructions for your composition and the length of each section. Analyze.

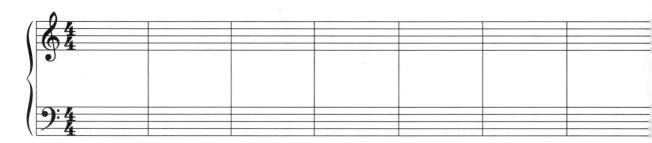

establish
tonic
contrapuntally

move to ♭VI
through passing
V$^4_3$/ ♭VI

establish ♭VI harmonically
for 2 – 3 mm. End up on
V^7/ ♭VI. Treat is as a Ger$^6_5$
and resolve to V–I in new key.

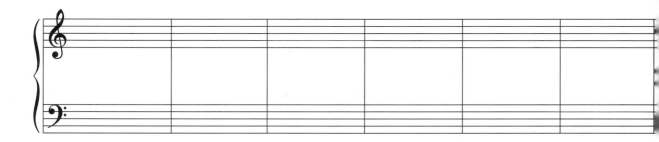

begin A2(D3/A 4) +app$^6_5$;
treat arrival as minor tonic

use D2(D5/A 4) to mod.
to III of this key.

expand +6 with V in this new k
end w/PAC. What key is this?

EXERCISE 27.28   Composition

Write a consequent phrase for each of the antecedent phrases below in order to create parallel progressive periods. Incorporate one example of ♭II and an augmented sixth chord in each consequent phrase. Analyze. In Example C, transform the four-measure chord progression into a twelve-measure composition by slowing the harmonic rhythm. This is easiest if you develop a motivic idea and create an accompanimental pattern from the homophonic chord progression. Consider appropriate metrical placement for the harmonies.

A.

B.

C.

CHAPTER 28

Ternary Form

EXERCISE 28.1   Analysis of Ternary and Binary Forms

Recall that there may be some ambiguity between a work cast in ternary form with transitions and retransitions and one that is written in rounded binary form. In order to compare and contrast these forms, numerous examples appear below. Some examples are unambiguous, while the forms of others could be argued as being either binary or ternary, depending on your own interpretation. Listen to and study each piece carefully in order to develop an interpretation. Then, make a formal diagram for each piece that includes the major sections, transitions, and retransitions. Leading questions accompany some examples. Finally, for each example, summarize your interpretation in a paragraph.

A.   Haydn, Trio, Piano Sonata in D major, Hob. XVI. 14

B. Chopin, Mazurka in E minor, op. 17, no. 2, BI 77

1. Discuss examples of the important role that unprepared dissonance plays
    in this piece.
2. Discuss the phrase period structure in mm. 1–12 and in mm. 12–24.
3. What is the underlying harmonic motion in mm. 1–12?
4. The material in mm. 25ff. contrasts with the material in the first section.
    One could argue, however, that many of the melodic gestures could be
    traced back to the first section. Support this assertion with examples; in
    particular, focus on the opening tune of the *dolce* section and the chromatic
    material over the G pedal that follows.
5. Are there transitions and retransitions? If so, cite specific locations.

(Continued)

(*Continued*)

C. Beethoven, Bagatelle No. 8 in G minor, op. 119, no. 1

1. How many phrases occur in mm. 1–16? Do they combine to form one or
    more periods?

2. There is an interesting relationship between mm. 1–4 and mm. 5–8. Dis-
    cuss. (Hint: Study the relationship between the hands.)

3. Given the prominence of the upper-neighbor figure, 5–6–5, might this
    be viewed as a motive? Trace other statements of this figure—on both
    the surface and below the surface (i.e., migration to the bass and har-

monic structure)—and/or any other motivic ideas that you may find interesting.

D. Haydn, *Menuetto: Allegro*, String Quartet in F major, op. 74, no. 2, Hob. III. 73

1. Provide a two-level harmonic analysis that details (a) the deepest-level tonal relations of the movement and (b) tonicizations within formal sections.

2. What type of period opens the movement? How many phrases are there? How are they linked harmonically?

3. The chromaticism that appears in m. 4 is striking, almost shocking. Haydn often injects chromaticism into the opening of a piece, and, as we have

seen in the work of other composers, the chromaticism appears throughout the movement, and may be often developed in ways that help to explain unusual tonal relations as simply harmonizations, and thus stabilizations, of chromatic pitches. Explore the reappearance of such chromaticism.

4. What function does the material in mm. 28–41 play? What would be a good label for this section?
5. Label and discuss the tonal functions of sequential passages.

(Continued)

(*Continued*)

EXERCISE 28.2   Analysis and Dictation

This exercise is identical to the previous exercise, except that the bass lines are omitted from areas of some examples. Notate the missing bass notes by listening and by the implications of the given upper voices. Further, analyze each piece in its entirety. In addition, provide a complete formal label that includes subsections and accompanying harmonic areas and in a sentence or two, support your choice of form with relevant examples. Finally, answer any accompanying questions.

A.   Schumann, "Albumblätter, I," *Bunte Blätter*, op. 99
Brahms later used this small piece as the theme for a set of variations for piano solo. What type of phrase period structure occurs in mm. 1–8 and 17–24? Could this piece be viewed as a binary form? Discuss.

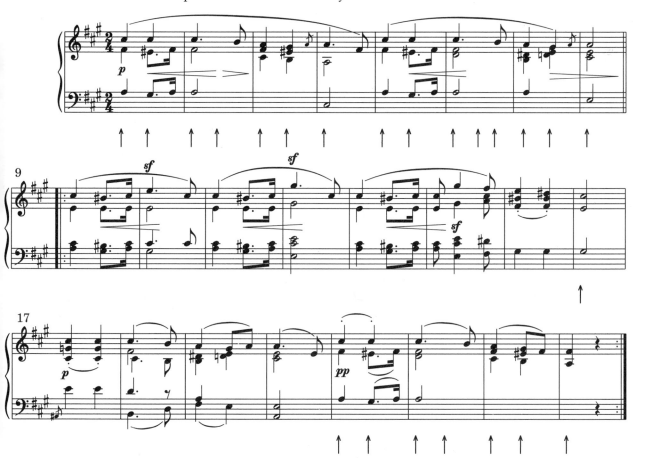

B.   Mozart, Menuetto, from Serenade in D major, for Strings and Winds, K. 250 ("Haffner"). What harmonic technique occurs in 9ff (label precisely)? Does any of the chromaticism presented in these measures reappear later, and if so, where?

C. Brahms, Waltz in E minor, *Waltzes for Piano*, op. 39, no. 4
What type of phrase structure occurs in mm. 1–8?

D. Bach, "Bete aber auch dabei" ("Yet Pray, Even While"), *Mache dich mein Geist bereit (Get Prepared, My Soul)*, BWV 115

Bete aber auch dabei	Yet pray, even while
Mitten in dem Wachen!	in the middle of keeping watch!
Bitte bei der grossen Schuld	In your great guilt
Deinen Richter um Geduld	beg the Judge for patience
Soll er dich von Sünden frei	and He shall free them from sin
Und gereinigt machen!	and make you cleansed

1. What contrapuntal technique is primary in this aria? Mark specific instances on the score.
2. The upper-neighbor figure is prevalent throughout the movement to a degree that we might consider it to be a motive. Focusing on the figure that

occurs on $\hat{5}$ and $\hat{6}$, mark instances of it in the opening ritornello, then summarize in a paragraph where and how this motive appears in different harmonic contexts throughout the aria.

3. What is the primary key in mm. 25–40? What secondary keys occur within these measures? Is there an underlying harmonic progression in mm. 25–40?

4. Bracket and label any sequences or sequential harmonic progressions in the aria.

(Continued)

(*Continued*)

(Continued)

(*Continued*)

Da Capo.

EXERCISE 28.3   Aural Identification and Analysis of Ternary and Binary Forms

We turn now to listening to and answering questions about ternary and binary forms without the aid of the score. Provide a formal diagram and formal label for each piece. Include subsections in your diagram. Support your answers carefully in a short paragraph. Answer any questions that accompany the individual pieces.

A.   Beethoven, Bagatelle No. 11 in A major, op. 119, no. 4
Provide a phrase period diagram for the first two phrases.

B.   Schumann, "Sizilianisch," *Album für die Jugend*, op. 68, no. 11
Cast in $\frac{6}{8}$ and a fairly rapid tempo, this piece begins in A minor. In what key are we at m. 8?

C. Schumann, "Widmung," ("Dedication"), op. 25
Translation:

Du meine Seele, du mein herz,	Oh you, my soul, oh you, my heart,
Du meine Wonn', o du mein Schmerz,	Oh you, my delight, oh you, my sorrow,
Du meine Welt, in der ich lebe,	Oh you, my world wherein I live,
mein Himmel du, darein ich schwebe,	You my heaven into which I soar,
O du mein Grab, in das hinab	Oh you my grave, wherein deep down
Ich ewig meinen Kummer gab!	Forever I have laid my sorrow!
Du bist die Ruh', du bist der Frieden;	You are the rest, you are the peace;
Du bist vom Himmel mir beschieden.	Heaven has destined you for me.
Dass du mich liebst, macht mich mir wert,	That you love me makes me deem myself worth,
Dein Blich hat mich vor mir verklärt	Your gaze has transfigured me to myself,
Du hebst mich liebend über mich,	Your love lifts me above myself,
Mein guter Geist, mein bess'res ich!	My good spirit, my better self!
Du meine Seele, du mein Herz,	You my soul, you my heart,
Du meine Wonn', o du mein Schmerz,	You my delight, oh you, my sorrow,
Du meine Welt, in der ich lebe,	You my world wherein I live,
Mein Himmel du, darein ich schwebe,	My heaven you, into which I soar,
Mein guter Geist, mein bessres ich!	My good spirit, my better self!

1. In what key does the first large section close?
2. The following highly contrasting section is in a chromatically third-related key. What key is it?
3. What type of modulation is used (common chord, common tone or unprepared)?
4. Below is the score for the end of a contrasting section of the piece and the beginning of a new section. Study the score carefully and provide roman numerals; then, in a few sentences, describe precisely what happens harmonically. Focus on the music that sets the text "verklärt, du hebst mich liebend" ("transfigured, your love lifts me"). Could this have influenced what Schumann did harmonically here?

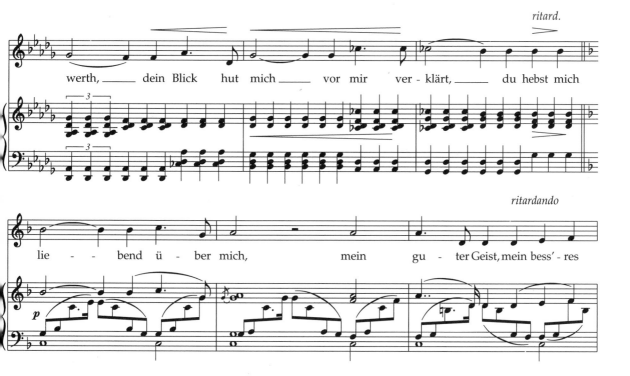

D.   Schumann, "Winterzeit I," *Album für die Jugend,* op. 68, no. 38
Below is an incomplete score for mm. 1–5. Notate the missing bass line.

EXERCISE 28.4   Play and Sing

Study each two-voice example and determine a logical implied progression. Then, be able to sing either voice while playing the other. Transpose each progression as shown for at least two repetitions.

A.

B.

C.

CHAPTER 29

Rondo

EXERCISE 29.1   Analysis

Listen to and study the scores, make form diagrams, and answer the following questions.

A.   Haydn, *Finale: Presto, ma non troppo,* Piano Sonata No. 50 in D major, Hob. XVI. 37

1. The sectional character of this rondo is enhanced by nested forms that are either ternary or binary types. Label the specific type of these nested forms.
2. Discuss any changes that occur in the restatements of the refrain.
3. One could view the material that begins in m. 28 to be derived from earlier material. Explore this possibility.

FINALE
Presto ma non troppo

(Continued)

(*Continued*)

B. Beethoven, *Allegro,* String Quartet No. 4 in C minor, op. 18, no. 4

1. What is the form of the opening refrain? What is the period structure of the A section within the refrain?
2. What harmonic procedure occurs in the B section of the refrain?
3. In spite of the fact that two different chords are involved, the pre-dominant in m. 15 encompasses two beats; discuss how these chords are related.
4. What contrapuntal technique occurs in the first episode? (Hint: What is the relationship between the instruments? You may wish to compare the opening second violin line with the first violin, cello, and viola lines.) Why might this relationship be easier to hear in the B section of the first episode?
5. What is the major difference between A1 and A2?
6. How would you support the assertion that the C section (the second episode) is derived from both the refrain and the B section?
7. How would you explain the two dozen or so measures that occur before the final *Prestissimo*?
8. List at least three ways that the material in the *Prestissimo* section summarizes material presented earlier in the movement.

(Continued)

(Continued)

(Continued)

(Continued)

Prestissimo.

EXERCISE 29.2   Aural Analysis

You will hear three rondos, for which no score is included. Answer the following questions and complete the tasks.

A. Beethoven, *Allegro comodo*, Piano Sonata No. 9 in E major, op. 14, no. 1

1. There is a transition between the refrain and the first episode; from what material is it derived?
2. There is a transition that moves to the C section. What crucial harmonic change occurs at the beginning of the transition and how does it help prepare the key of G major?
3. The key of the C section is G major. Is this unusual, and if so, why?
4. What rhythmic effect occurs in the final statement of the refrain?
5. Make a formal diagram that includes the prevailing key of each section. Make sure that you have already answered the previous questions, since they will guide your listening.

B. Beethoven, *Allegro*, Piano Sonata No. 8 in C minor, "Pathétique," op. 13

1. Notate mm. 1–8 of the soprano tune of the refrain.

2. Discuss the tonal and phrase/formal structure of the refrain. Consider modulations, sequences, and unusual phrase characteristics.
3. The B section is in a major key. What are Beethoven's most likely tonal possibilities based on your knowledge of rondo form?
4. What harmonic procedure occurs in the B section?
5. Below are the upper voices for a passage within the B section. Notate the missing bass voice and provide roman numerals (mm. 43–51).

6. Are there significant changes in repetitions of the refrain? Describe.

7. In what key is the C section? What contrapuntal technique characterizes this section?

8. Is this a five- or seven-part rondo? If it is seven, what changes occur in the repetition of the B section?

9. The closing measures of the movement are reproduced below. What formal label might you apply to this section? Provide roman numerals for these measures. Why might Beethoven have briefly tonicized the key that he does in mm. 200–206?

C. Beethoven, *Allegro,* Violin Sonata No. 1 in D major, op. 12, no. 1

1. Make a detailed formal chart of this movement that includes the key structure.

2. Below are the upper parts of the refrain. Listen to them, notate the bass, and provide roman numerals. What kind of period is this?

3. Which formal section is represented below? Notate the bass of the following four measures.

4. What important harmonic change takes place soon after the beginning of the second statement of the refrain? Be specific.
5. This change sets up the opening key of the C section. What is this key?
6. Below is an incomplete excerpt from near the end of the movement (the bass line is missing). What formal section does this immediately follow? How is the musical material deployed between the violin and the piano in this excerpt? What is this technique called?

(Continued)

(*Continued*)

7. Fill in the missing bass notes and provide roman numerals for the entire excerpt. Be aware that there is a very important harmonic change that occurs in the bass line descent; the initial statement is labeled "x," and the altered statement is labeled "y." What exactly is changed?

8. What effect does this change at "y" and the following measures have on the harmonic structure?

EXERCISE 29.3   Potpourri of Aural Analysis of Binary, Rondo, and Ternary Forms

You will hear six movements; no scores are included, except for excerpts that accompany specific questions. Answer the following questions.

A. Haydn, *Finale,* Piano Sonata in D major, Hob. XVI. 19

   1. Make a formal diagram below that includes important key areas.
   2. Does recurrence of material remain the same or change?

B. Haydn, *Menuetto: Allegro,* String Quartet in G minor, op. 20, no. 3, Hob. III. 33

   1. Make a formal diagram that includes important keys.
   2. Below is the incomplete score of mm. 1–10. Notate the bass, give roman numerals, and then make a phrase period diagram.

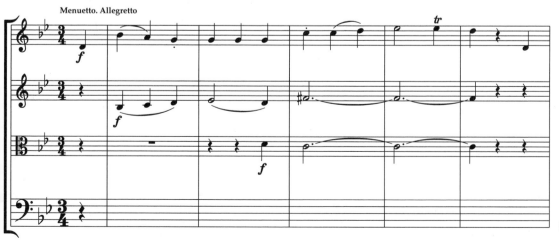

(*Continued*)

(Continued)

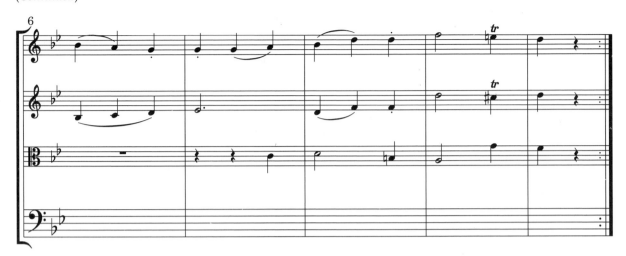

3. What contrapuntal device does Haydn employ later in this large section?
4. Below is the music that occurs near the close of the first large section. Notate the bass and provide roman numerals.

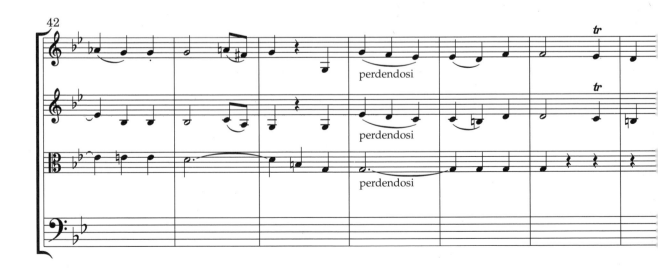

5. Below is the music that occurs near the end of another formal section. Notate the bass. What is the harmonic technique in this excerpt?

C. Schumann, *Kreisleriana,* op. 16, no. 3

   1. Make a detailed formal diagram that includes the form and keys of any subsections.

   2. What harmonic technique occurs in the opening section of the piece?

D. Mozart, *Allegro,* Sonata No. 3 in A major for Flute and Piano, K. 12

   1. Make a formal diagram.

   2. Make a phrase period diagram of the opening period (the meter is $\frac{3}{8}$, felt as one beat per measure).

   3. The material that follows the opening period is closely related to the opening material, yet is deployed differently; discuss.

E. Schubert, *Allegro vivace,* String Quartet No. 11 in E major, op. 125, no. 2, D. 353

   1. Make a formal diagram.

   2. Make a phrase period diagram for mm. 1–12. Discuss unusual features.

   3. What chromatic harmony is tonicized in the following section? (Hint: Com-

pare the opening sonority of that section with the end of the preceding section; focus on the motion in the cello part.)

F.   Beethoven, *Allegro assai*, Piano Sonata No. 3 in C major, op. 2, no. 3

1. Make a formal diagram that includes important keys.
2. Do mm. 1–8 form a period? Support your answer.
3. Below is the incomplete score from the opening of which formal section? Notate the bass line and provide roman numerals.

EXERCISE 29.4   Composition

A.   Write two consequent phrases to the given antecedent below. The result will be a double period. The first consequent should close on V. After repeating the given antecedent, the second consequent should close in the tonic. Then, write a solo melody that will be performed above your homophonic accompaniment. Analyze.

B.   Complete the excerpt below, which is in nineteenth-century mazurka style, by doing the following:

1. Realize the remaining figured bass for the eight-measure phrase.
2. Continue the melody that was started.
3. Write an appropriate eight-measure consequent phrase to create a PIP.
4. Analyze each harmony and provide a second-level analysis.

CHAPTER 30

Sonata Form

EXERCISE 30.1   Analysis

Below is a movement cast in sonata form. Listen to it and then make a formal diagram that includes the location, name, and key of each section. Finally, answer the series of questions that follows the score.

(Continued)

(Continued)

(Continued)

(Continued)

A. Beethoven, *Allegro*, Piano Sonata No. 1 in F minor, op. 2, no. 1

1. Although this is Beethoven's first piano sonata with an opus (he wrote several earlier sonatas while in Bonn), it has many unusual events. For example, the FTA can be viewed as being exceptionally short, while the beginning of the STA might be considered to balance the short FTA by its considerable length. Discuss these and other unusual features of this sonata.

2. Beethoven builds remarkable energy in mm. 1–8. Discuss how he accomplishes this by focusing on harmonic rhythm.

3. E♮ is left conspicuously hanging in m. 8. Some composers, including Beethoven, created connections between phrases and even sections of a work by endowing specific pitches with associative power. Explore this possibility in this movement beginning with the E♮⁵.

4. What type of sequence appears in the transition? Where is the first authentic cadence in the STA? Is this unusual?

5. There are several sequences in the development. Label each.

6. One might view most of the development to lie in the key of A♭ (III). Given this, list any keys that Beethoven tonicizes in relation to A♭. Does A♭ lead directly to the retransition, or is there another key that links A♭ and the retransition's dominant?

7. This sonata illustrates how an initial surface motive can control almost all of the movement's subsequent melodic and harmonic material. Below is a reduction of mm. 1 through 8.

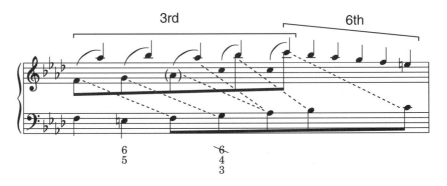

The opening ascending arpeggiation in the right hand moves to A♭⁵, followed by a turn figure around F. It is repeated a step higher and moves to B♭ followed by a turn around G. A♭⁵ (m. 5) and the B♭⁵ (m. 6) are both marked *sforzando* and ascend to the C (m. 7), which is marked *fortissimo*. This ascent to C is balanced by a descent of a sixth from C⁶ to the hanging E♮⁵.

Might this motivic sixth from the FTA also occur in other formal sections of the sonata? You may wish to look not only at the surface of thematic events, but also at any lines that occur below the surface, such as between the beginning and ending points of sequences. You might even wish to explore the development for the opening motive's deep-level repetition, a feature that we also saw in Mozart's B♭ major sonata. Do not ignore rhythmic correspondences.

The bass voice exhibits a melodic pattern in mm. 1–8. F³ is prolonged by its lower neighbor, E♮³, before it rises to C⁴ by stepwise motion. In fact, this same fifth ascent is manifested in the upper voice, by the F⁴ (m. 1) moving to G⁴ (m. 3), to A♭⁴ (m. 5), to B♭⁴ (m. 6), and finally to C⁵ (m. 7). We can now understand that by delaying the ascent in the bass for one measure, the neighboring V⁶₅, (m. 3) transforms what would have been parallel octaves resulting from the fifth ascent between the two voices into a canon between the two voices.

EXERCISE 30.2   Analysis and Dictation

This exercise requires you to perform the same tasks as in the previous exercise. In addition, there are a few "bare spots" in the music, areas where the score is incomplete (either the bass line or the entire passage is missing). Notate the bass line for these areas marked with brackets.

A. Mozart, *Allegro*, Piano Sonata in F major, K. 332

(Continued)

(Continued)

(Continued)

(*Continued*)

(Continued)

(*Continued*)

1. F major is explicit in the movement's first phrase, but what other key is implied?
2. What contrapuntal and metric techniques occur in mm. 5 to 9?
3. What key is implied at the beginning of the transition? What about at the end of the transition? What key actually occurs at the STA?

4. What harmonic technique occurs in mm. 60–65? (Identification of this technique will aid in notating the missing bass line.)

5. What is the motivic relationship between the FTA theme and the theme in mm. 86–88?

6. Explore thematic/motivic relationships between mm. 89–93 and the opening two measures of the development.

7. What key is strongly implied in mm. 118 to 126? Is this key ever realized?

8. Does anything unusual occur in the FTA and the STA of the recapitulation? If so, describe.

B. Mozart, *Allegro,* Clarinet Quintet in A major, K. 581
Note: Clarinet in A sounds a minor third lower than written.

1. The FTA begins with the strings and the clarinet almost at odds. That is, the strings are a unified group that presents the initial tunes, while the clarinet seems to play a subordinate role, only commenting on the strings' material, rather than presenting thematic material. Do you think that the strings play a more primary role throughout the movement, or does the clarinet begin to gain importance at some point? Develop the idea of a possible conflict versus interaction between strings and the clarinet.

2. A glance at the opening string gestures reveals a highly contrapuntal texture governed by contrary motion. In fact, the end points of the opening contrary-motion gestures (mm. 2 and 4) are on $\hat{6}$ (vi), creating the effect that the submediant harmony is preventing typical closure on the tonic (that is, $\hat{5}$ moves to $\hat{6}$, rather than to $\hat{1}$). It is only in the third attempt to cadence that Mozart succeeds in an authentic cadence (m. 7), though the clarinet enters at that moment, weakening the tonic arrival by creating a phrase overlap. Explore the specific idea that various forms of deceptive motions stemming from $\hat{5}$–$\hat{6}$ create drama throughout this movement. You may wish to discuss the more general 5–6 neighbor motion that also seems to play an important role both melodically and harmonically. Summarize your results in a paragraph or two, supporting your view with specific examples.

3. Bracket and label all sequential motions in the movement. Does one sequence type occur more often than the others? If so, can you trace the melodic motion of the sequence to the opening motivic gestures that were discussed in question 2?

4. Modal mixture is arguably the most important chromatic technique used in this movement. Identify at least four instances of mixture, making sure you include both local (surface) statements and deeper-level (tonal) statements. What contrapuntal technique generates many of these instances of mixture?

(Continued)

(Continued)

(Continued)

(*Continued*)

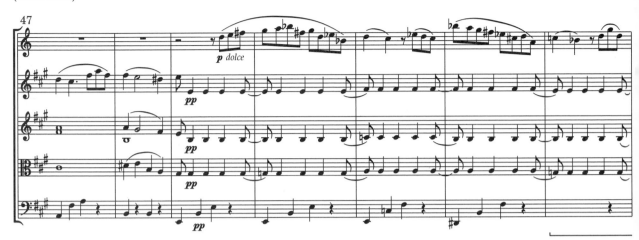

(Continued)

(*Continued*)

(Continued)

(*Continued*)

(Continued)

(*Continued*)

(Continued)

(*Continued*)

EXERCISE 30.3   Aural Analysis

You will hear three sonata movements; however, no scores are provided. There are two types of tasks in this exercise. The first task requires you to answer a series of questions similar to those above that will accompany each movement. The second task is new and will accompany the second and third examples. It involves identifying formal sections and their keys. As you listen to the movements, numbers will be called out that represent points in the formal structure. You should answer the questions that correspond to these numbers. In general, you will be asked, "Where are we in the form?" and you will respond with an answer such as "STA." There may be additional questions.

A.   Mozart, *Allegro maestoso,* Piano Sonata in A minor, K. 310

Exposition:

1.   What type of sequence is implied in the FTA?
2.   Name the type of transition. Near the end of the transition, what unusual key is implied? Be specific.
3.   In what key is the STA? Is this a monothematic sonata?
4.   Is there a closing section? If so, how many subsections occur within the closing section?

Development:

5.   What key opens the development? What thematic material is used in this section?
6.   The development is composed of two giant sequences. What types are they? Be careful—the first sequence is quite spread out.
7.   What harmony immediately precedes the V of the retransition and continues to expand V within the retransition?

Recapitulation:

8.   Compare the opening of the transition in the recapitulation to the opening of the transition in the exposition. Describe the difference in texture between these two places.
9.   In what key is the STA of the recapitulation?
10. If there is a closing section in the recapitulation, compare it to the exposition: are there any significant changes in the recapitulation's closing section (other than the obvious transposition to the tonic)?

B.   Haydn, *Allegro,* String Quartet in G minor, "Horseman," op. 74, no. 3, Hob. III. 74
Answer the following questions based on the number called out:

1.   Where are we in the form?
2.   What rhythmic effect is taking place here?
3.   Where are we in the form and in what key?
4.   Where are we in the form?
5.   What harmonic progression is this?
6.   What harmonic progression is this?
7.   Where are we in the form? Is there anything unusual about it? If so, how would this impact the way you would analyze the opening of the movement?
8.   Where and what key are we in the form?

Short-answer questions:

1.   The opening eight-measure "gallop" has a three-chord harmonic progression; using roman numerals, write down the chords.
2.   What contrapuntal technique does Haydn use in the next phrase?
3.   Comparing the harmonic content of these two phrases, what strikes you as very similar?
4.   Is there a closing section in the exposition?
5.   In what key does the exposition close?
6.   In what key does the development begin? How long does this key last?
7.   What thematic material is used in the development?
8.   Discuss at least one unusual feature that occurs near the close of the development.
9.   Are there significant differences between the exposition's transition and that which occurs in the recap? If so, what are they?

C.   Haydn, *Allegro assai,* Symphony No. 45 in F♯ minor, "Farewell Symphony," Hob. I. 45
In mm. 1–16 (essentially one large phrase) the harmony changes every two measures except for a couple of spots: Identify each harmony in the blanks provided.

mm.	1–2	3–4	5–6	7–8	9	10	11–12	13	14	15–16
	—	—	—	—	—	—	—	—	—	—

1.   Name the formal segment. What key is it in?
2.   Name the formal segment. What key does it begin in?
3.   Name the formal segment. What key is it in? What is the origin of this material?
4.   Name the formal segment. Has this been heard before and if so, how does it differ from its earlier appearance?
5.   Name the formal segment. What is unusual about it and why?
6.   What type of transition occurs in the exposition? To what tonal area does it lead? A sequence appears in it; what type?
7.   In what tonal area does the exposition close?
8.   How long is the retransition?

CHAPTER 31

New Harmonic Tendencies

EXERCISE 31.1 Analysis

The excerpts below contain ambiguities resulting from modal mixture, semitonal voice leading, the reciprocal process, and enharmonic puns. Bracket the area or areas in which tonal ambiguity occurs. Label the type of ambiguity and answer any accompanying questions.

A. Wagner, *Das Rheingold*, act I, scene 3

(Alberich demonstrates the magical powers of the Tarnhelm.) In what key is this example? Is there a functional harmonic progression? Begin by looking at the excerpt's close.

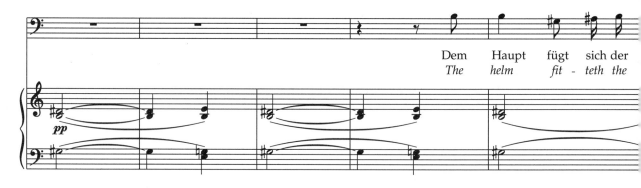

Dem Haupt fügt sich der Helm: The helm fits the head
ob sich der Zauber auch zeigt?   Now will the magic also appear?
"Nacht und Nebel . . .   "Night and Fog . . .

B. Beethoven, *Vivace* and *Presto*, Symphony No. 7 in A major, op. 92
Below are two excerpts from Beethoven's Seventh Symphony. The first excerpt begins on V/A. What key succeeds A major and how is it secured? The second excerpt also illustrates a tonal motion. Compare and contrast the two methods of tonicization.

C. Brahms, "Mein Herz ist schwer" ("My Heart is Heavy"), op. 94, no. 3
This song is in G minor; discuss the tonic's strength and function at the piece's close.

Herz ____ ist schwer, ___ mein Au - ge wacht,   mein

(Continued)

(*Continued*)

      . . . Mein Herz ist schwer, mein Auge   . . . My heart is heavy, my eyes are
wach.   awake.

EXERCISE 31.2   Dictation

 Notate bass and soprano voices and provide a roman numeral analysis. Finally, in a few sentences describe the type of ambiguity involved.

A.

B.

C. Brahms, "An die Nachtigall" ("To the Nightingale"), op. 46, no. 4

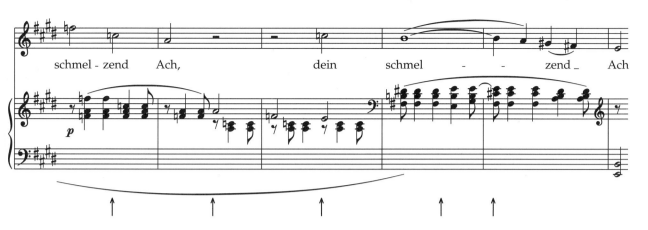

Du tönest mir mit deiner süssen Kehle

Die Liebe wach;
Denn schon durchbebt die Tiefen
    meiner Seele
Dein schmelzend >>Ach<<

With your sweet throat, you call me
    and
Awaken Love within me;
Because the depths of my soul are
    already stirred
By your melting cry.

D.   Beethoven, *Allegro molto,* Symphony No. 2 in D major, op. 36
Provide missing bass notes and add one additional chord to the end to resolve
the bass.

EXERCISE 31.3   Figured Basses

Figured bass A below reviews traditional chromaticism. Figured bass B contains
various plagal relations. Construct a good soprano for figured bass A; fill in in-

ner voices for both A and B. Include a second-level analysis that reflects the large-scale harmonic progression in figured bass A.

A.

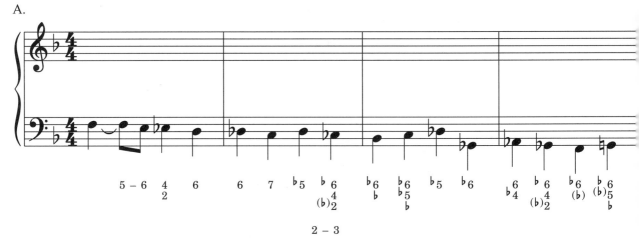

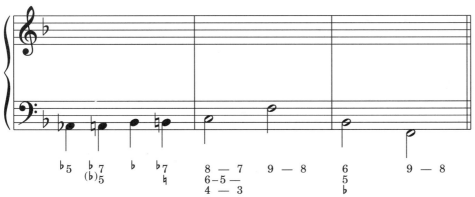

B.

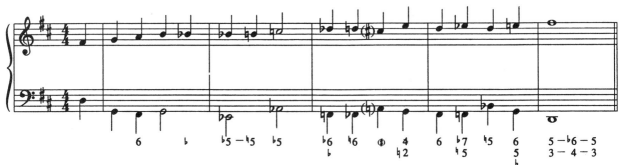

EXERCISE 31.4   Keyboard: Warm-Up and Review (I)

Complete the tasks below.

A.   Modulate from E major to ♭III using modal mixture in the home key to prepare the new key. You may write out a basic sketch of what you will be playing. Analyze your work. Also include the following in your example:

1.   a D2 (D5/A4) or A2 (D3/A4) sequence in either key. You may use either a diatonic or an applied chord sequence.
2.   a tonicization of the Neapolitan
3.   an expansion of the pre-dominant area in ♭III that includes both the Ger $\frac{6}{5}$ and Ger °3 chord.

B.   Add inner voices to the unfigured bass and soprano melody below. Analyze and transpose to one other key of your choice.

EXERCISE 31.5   Keyboard: Warm-up and Review (II)

Continue the progressions below based on the pivot chord instructions. Transpose to two other keys of your choice.

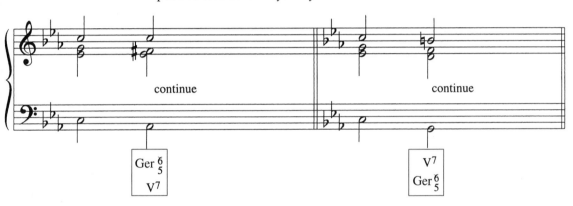

EXERCISE 31.6   Keyboard: Warm-up and Review (III)

Realize and analyze the figured bass in four-voice keyboard style.

EXERCISE 31.7   Analysis of Enharmonically Reinterpreted Diminished Seventh Chords

Mark the pivot in the examples below which modulate using an enharmonically reinterpreted diminished seventh chord.

A.

B.

C.   Wolf, "Verschling' der Abgrund meines Liebsten Hütte" ("May the Abyss Swallow Up My Beloved's Cottage"), *Italienisches Liederbuch,* no. 45

Verschling der Abgrund meines Liebsten
Hütte,

May the abyss swallow up my
beloved's cottage

D.

E.

(Continued)

(*Continued*)

F.   Wagner, Overture, *Der fliegende Holländer* (The Flying Dutchman), act I.

G.   Beethoven, *Larghetto,* Symphony No. 2 in D major, op. 36
Begin by finding cadences. Then determine how the reinterpreted diminished seventh secures the key.

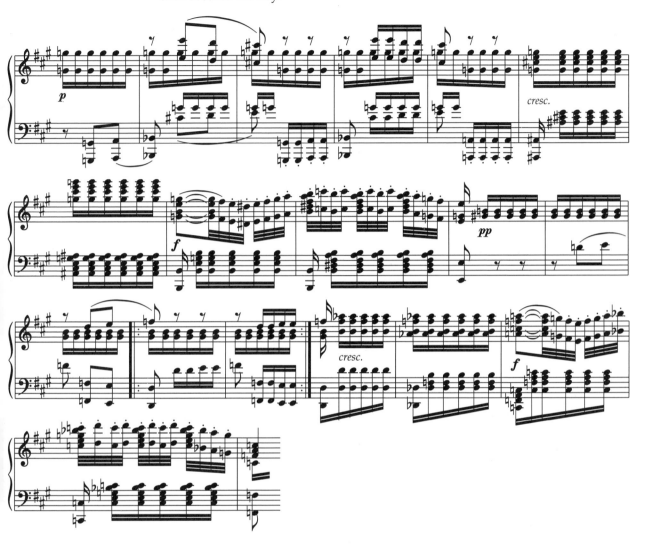

EXERCISE 31.8   Figured Bass

Realize the figured bass below in four voices. It includes at least one and perhaps more enharmonic modulations using the diminished seventh chord. Then, be able to sing either the bass or the soprano voice while playing the other three voices on the piano. Analyze.

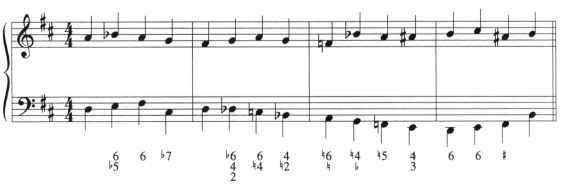

EXERCISE 31.9   Analysis and Dictation

Determine the goals of harmonic motion for the modulating passages below. Note values below the staff indicate harmonic rhythm. Then, notate the bass and soprano and provide roman numerals. Expect both diatonic and mixture pivots as well as enharmonic diminished sevenths. Label tones of figuration using figured bass notation. Finally, add logical inner voices, focusing on enharmonic diminished sevenths.

A.

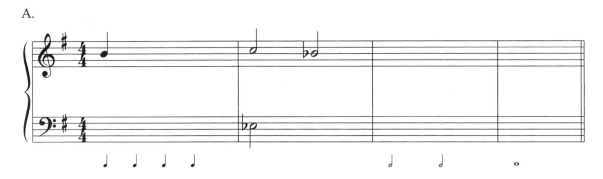

B.

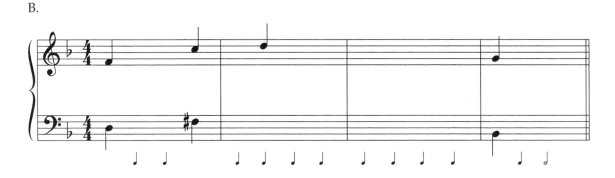

C.

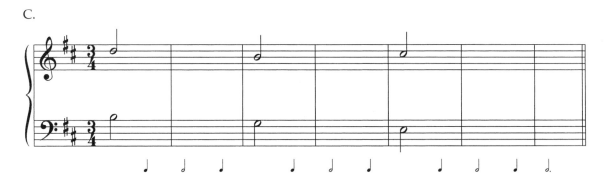

D.

E.

F.

EXERCISE 31.10   Dictation

 Notate bass and soprano in the progressions that modulate by enharmonic diminished sevenths. Analyze, marking the pivot carefully. Begin by determining the new key, then work backward from the cadence until you encounter the diminished seventh chord. Hint: A diminished seventh chord will often appear twice, first in its usual diatonic context, and then later in its enharmonic "chameleon-like" guise in order to prepare the new key.

A.

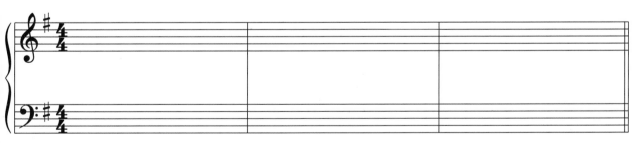

B.

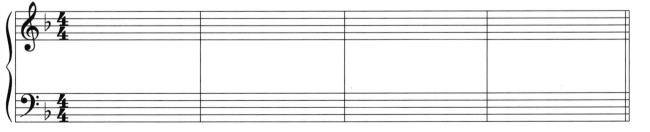

C.

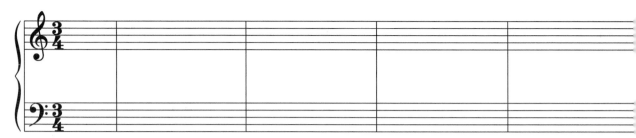

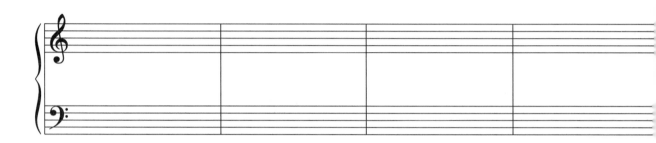

EXERCISE 31.11   Dictation

 Listen to and notate the outer voices of examples that modulate using the three types of pivot chords that we have discussed: diatonic, mixture, and enharmonic. Provide roman numerals and interpret the pivot chord. The possible tonal destinations are:

in major: ii, ♭II, iii, IV, V, ♭VI, vi, VI; in minor: III, iv, v, VI.

A.

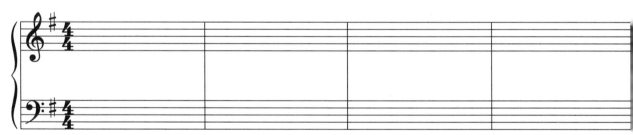

B.

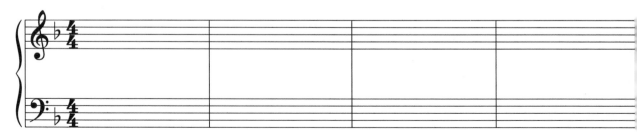

C.

D.

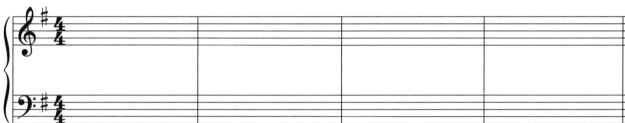

E.

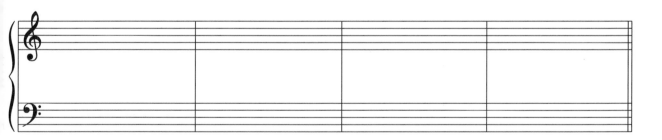

F.

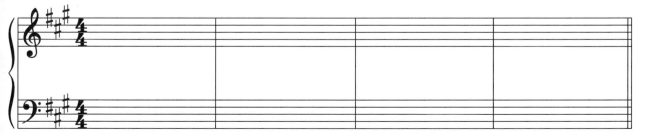

EXERCISE 31.12 Figured Bass

Realize the figured basses below, each of which contains an enharmonic modulation using the diminished seventh chord. Analyze, including the pivot chords.

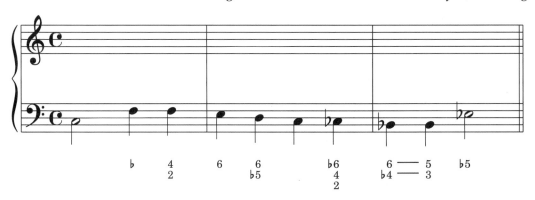

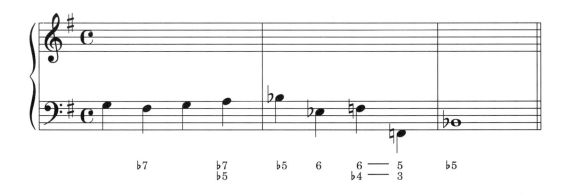

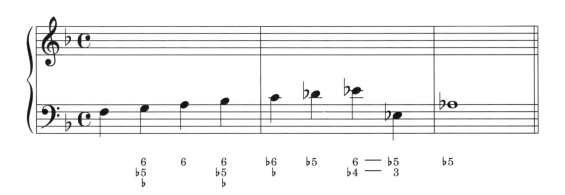

EXERCISE 31.13 Keyboard: Enharmonic Modulation Using Diminished Seventh Chords

1. Use the diminished seventh chord D–F–A♭–C♭ to modulate from E♭ major to C major.
2. Interpret each member of the diminished seventh chord C♯–E–G–B♭ as a root that leads to its own tonic. Be able to spell the chord correctly in each of the four keys. Then, play a progression that begins in one of the keys and includes the diminished seventh as a pivot that leads to one of the other distantly related keys.

EXERCISE 31.14   Keyboard

Study the following examples that enharmonically reinterpret a diminished seventh chord to modulate to distant keys. Then, play the short progressions and specify to which key the diminished seventh leads. Finally, play longer progressions (*c.* six to eight chords) that establish the initial key, C major. Modulate using the diminished seventh chord and close with a strong cadence in the new key.

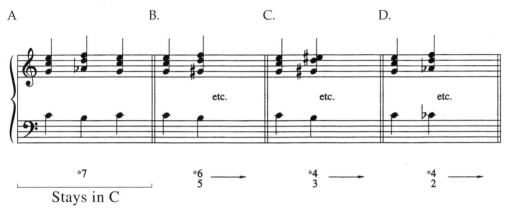

EXERCISE 31.15   Analysis

Below are examples that do not begin on the tonic. Study each carefully, determining how best to interpret their off-tonic structures within the overall key scheme.

A.   Schubert, Waltz, *12 Ländler,* op. 171, no. 4, D. 790

B.   Schubert, Waltz, *18 German Dances and Ecossaises,* op. 33, no. 5, D. 783

(Continued)

(*Continued*)

C.   Mendelssohn, "Wedding March," *Midsummer's Night Dream,* op. 61

D.   Wolf, "Nein, junger Herr" (No, Young Sir"), *Italienisches Liederbuch,* no. 12

Lebhaft und mit Grazie. (♪ = 152.)

Nein,   jun - ger Herr,   so   treibt man's nicht, für wahr;   man sorgt da -

Nein, junger Herr, so treibt man's nicht, fürwahr;
Man sorgt dafür

No young sir, one doesn't do such things, really,
one takes care

E.   Schubert, Waltz, *Letze waltzer*, op. 127, no. 15, D. 146

F.   Lamm, "Saturday in the Park"

EXERCISE 31.16   Composition

Using an enharmonically reinterpreted diminished seventh chord, write a modulating consequent phrase to the given antecedent phrase. Note that the diminished seventh chord is prepared in the antecedent phrase. Analyze, and play your solution.

CHAPTER 32

The Rise of Symmetrical Harmony in Tonal Music

EXERCISE 32.1 Analysis

Analyze the examples below that contain augmented triads and altered dominant seventh chords. Determine whether the dissonant pitches are tones of figuration (usually passing tones) or whether they are chordal members. Use figured bass notation. Passing tones are represented by a horizontal line (e.g., "$\hat{5}$—$\sharp\hat{5}$"). Chromatic alterations of chord members are shown by placing the alterations before the arabic numbers.

For example: V_7 or V_7
$\sharp5$ $\flat5$

A.

B.

C.

D. The ending of this exercise is tonally ambiguous. Discuss.

E. Schumann, "Fabel" ("Fable"), *Phantasiestückem*, op. 12, no. 6
Be aware that this excerpt does not begin in the tonic.

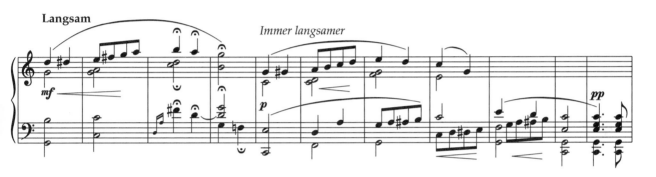

F. Beethoven, Variation XIV, *Diabelli Variations*, op. 120
Suspensions create the dissonant harmony that appears on the downbeat of m. 3.

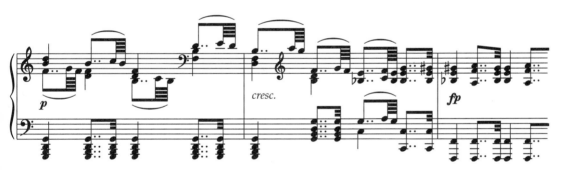

G. Brahms, "Unbewegte laue Luft" ("Motionless, Tepid Air"), op. 57, no. 8

(Continued)

(*Continued*)

Unbewegte laue Luft,   Motionless, tepid air,
Tiefe Ruhe der Natur; . . .   Nature, deeply at rest; . . .

EXERCISE 32.2   Analysis and Dictation

 Below are the upper parts of examples. Listen to and study what is given, then notate the bass and provide a roman numeral analysis.

A.

B.

C.

D. Beethoven, Bagatelle No. 8 in G minor, op. 119, no. 1

E. Haydn, *Andante grazioso,* String Quartet in G minor, op. 74, no. 2, Hob. III. 74

F. Schumann, *Scherzo, Klavierstücke,* op. 32
Be aware that there is an enharmonic modulation.

EXERCISE 32.3   Analysis of Chromatic Common-Tone Harmonies

Be aware that diminished sevenths and augmented sixths may be used either as common-tone chords (in which they contrapuntally prolong an underlying harmony) or as functional chords (in which they participate in the harmonic progression (augmented sixths function as pre-dominants and diminished sevenths function as dominants). Employ a two-level analysis, making sure that you distinguish between contrapuntal and harmonic functions.

A.

B.

C.   Chopin, Nocturne in A♭ major, op. 32, no. 2, BI 106

D.   Brahms, "Salamander," op. 107, no. 2

tut,   die   hei - sse ___ Lie - be ___ tut.

. . . wohl wie mir kühlem Teufel   . . . just as on me, a cold devil,
Die heisse Liebe tut.   hot love operates.

E.   Brahms, *Allegro con brio*, Symphony No. 3 in F major, op. 90

EXERCISE 32.4   Writing Altered Triads and Seventh Chords

Complete the tasks in four voices.

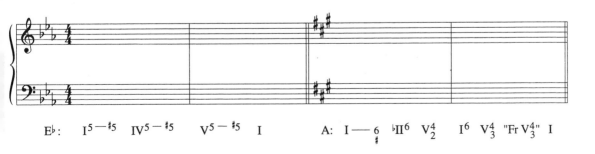

EXERCISE 32.5   Unfigured Bass

Add inner voices to create a four-voice texture. Use CT°7s where possible. Analyze.

tonic expansion

EXERCISE 32.6   Melody Harmonization

Set each soprano fragment in four voices, including at least one chromatic chord in each example. You may use modal mixture, applied chords, common-tone harmonies, altered dominant and dominant seventh chords, ♭II chords, and augmented sixth chords. Analyze. For Example E, include one of each of the following (but not necessarily in this order): altered dominant, applied dominant, V "Fr" $\frac{4}{3}$, and common-tone diminished seventh chord. Analyze.

A.

b:

B.

d:

C.

d:

D.

C in bass

E.

EXERCISE 32.7 Writing Common-Tone Harmonies

Use common-tone diminished sevenths to embellish tonic and dominant.

A.   B.   C.

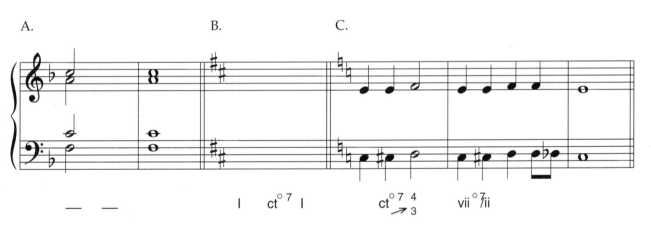

D.   E.   F.

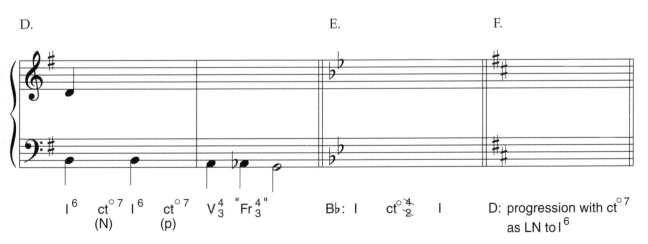

EXERCISE 32.8 Figured Basses

Realize the figured basses below in four voices. Analyze.

A.

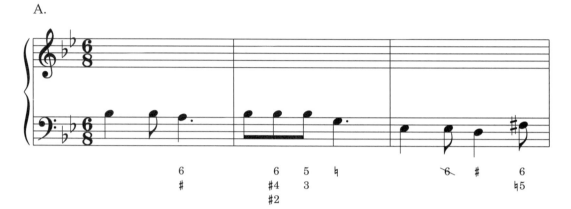

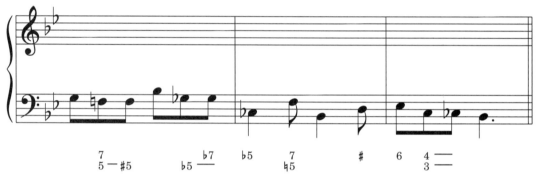

B.

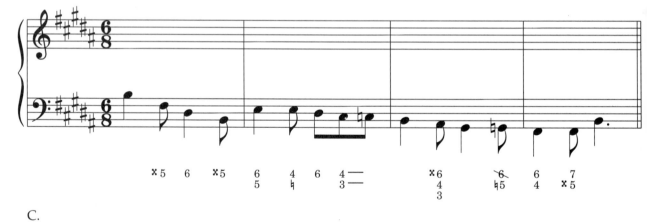

C.

EXERCISE 32.9   Analysis and Dictation

Notate the missing soprano or bass voice for the excerpts below that illustrate chromatically altered harmonies. Examples A–C focus on common-tone harmonies. Examples D–E include augmented triads, altered dominant seventh chords, and common-tone diminished seventh chords and augmented sixths. Add logical inner voices.

A.   B.

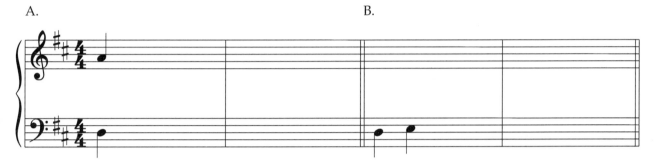

C.   Beethoven, Variation XII, *Diabelli Variations*, op. 120

D.

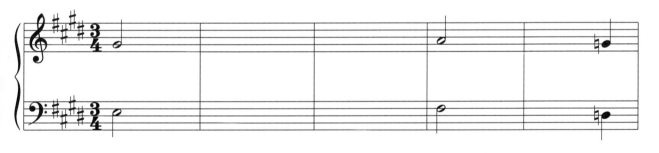

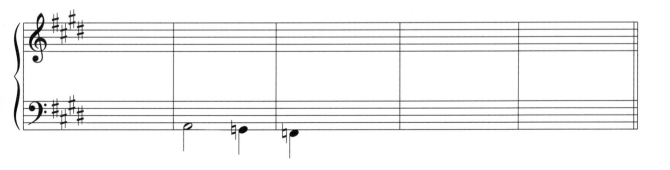

E.

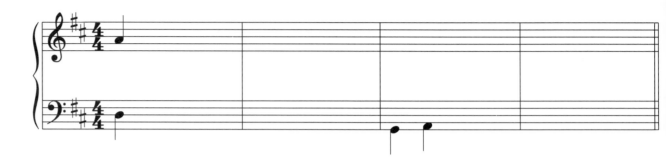

EXERCISE 32.10   Variations and Expansion of Harmonic Models

 You will hear two models, each of which is followed by a series of variations, or expansions on the model. On a separate piece of manuscript paper, notate the outer voices and provide a roman numeral analysis.

Model A

Expansion 1

Expansion 2

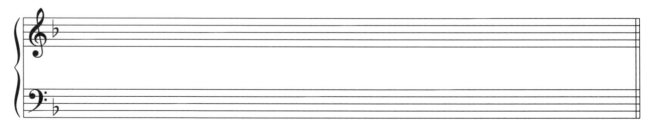

Expansion 3

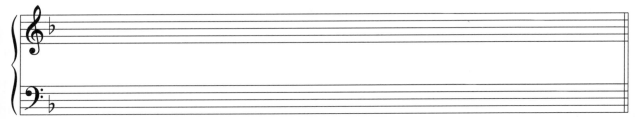

Expansion 4

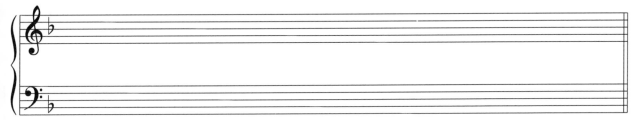

Model B

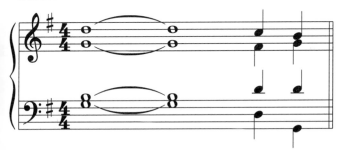

Expansion 1

Expansion 2

(Continued)

(*Continued*)

Expansion 3

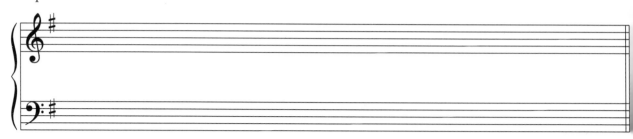

Expansion 4

Expansion 5

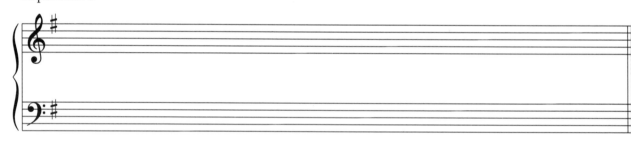

Expansion 6

Expansion 7

CHAPTER 33

Melodic and Harmonic Symmetry Combine: Chromatic Sequences

EXERCISE 33.1   Pattern Completion

Study the following sequential models, then write three copies. End with a strong cadence. Label each sequence type. Transpose each sequence to another key of your choice. Begin by writing the first of two-chord patterns, which must be consonant (major or minor) triads. Then add the helping (second) chord to each repetition.

A.

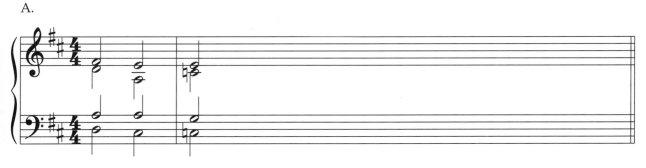

B.   Three voices only

C.   The model begins on beat 3

D.

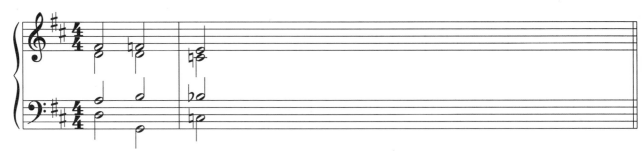

EXERCISE 33.2   Analysis of Chromatic Sequences

Bracket and label each sequence in the following exercises. Circle each bass note involved in the sequence. Do not analyze each harmony within the sequence. Rather, analyze the harmonies that begin and end the sequence, and then determine the underlying tonal progression.

A.   Carissimi, "Et ululantes filii Ammon" ("And Weeping, the Children of Ammon"), *Jephthah*

Slowly

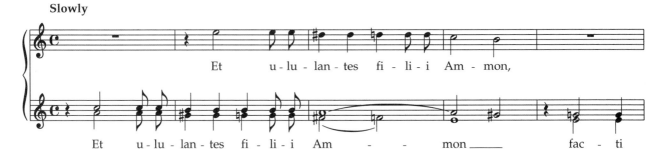

Et ululantes filii Ammon	And weeping, the children of Ammon
Facti sunt soram filis Israel	before the eyes of the children of Israel,
humiliati.	were subdued.

B.   Schubert, *Adagio molto—Allegro vivace*, Symphony No. 4 in C minor, "Tragic," D. 417

143

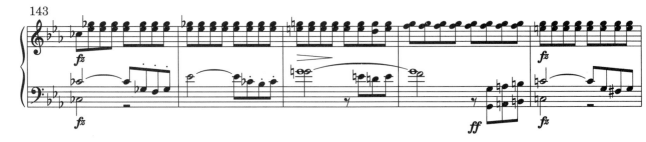

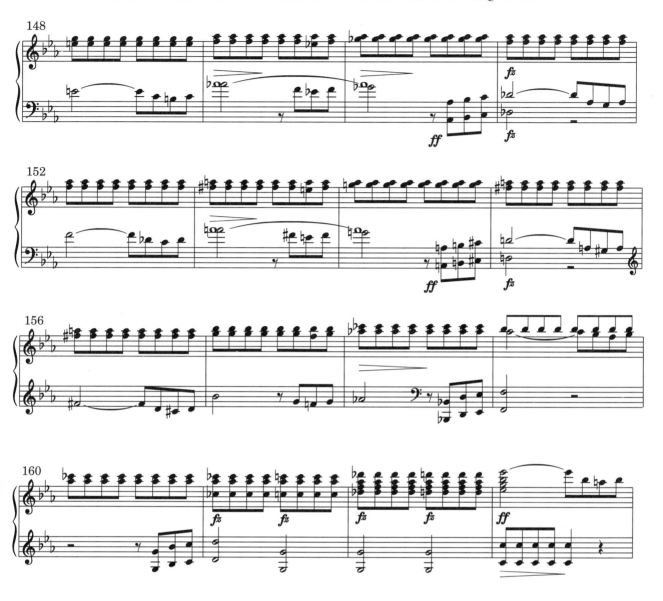

C. Schumann, *Andante un poco maestoso—Allegro molto vivace*, Symphony No. 1 in B♭ major, "Spring," op. 38

D.   Mendelssohn, Prelude in B minor, op. 104, no. 2

E.   Beethoven, *Menuetto,* Symphony No. 1 in C major, op. 21

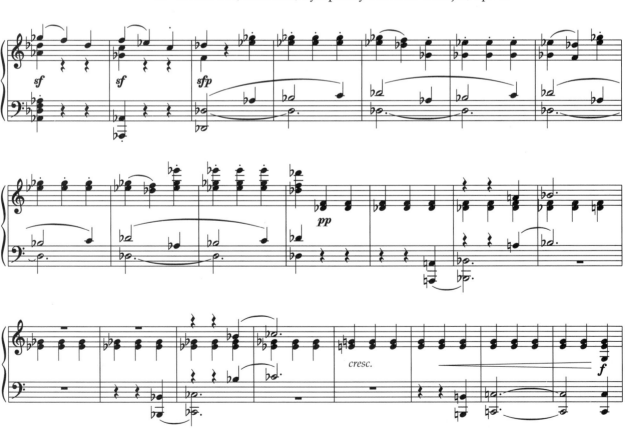

F.   The excerpts below from Chopin and Beethoven contain multiple sequences. Circle and label each.

1.   Chopin, *Allegro maestoso,* Piano Sonata in C minor, op. 4, BI 23

(Continued)

2. Beethoven, *Allegro,* Piano Concerto No. 1 in C major, op. 15

G. Donizetti, "Esci fuggi" Lucia di Lammermoor, Act II, scene 5

tà, sì,   quan - te   vol - te jad un   so - lo tor - men - to
thral, ah,   heav'n - ly   love hath a   balm for thy sor - row,

drà, sì,   sì,   la   mac - chia d'ol - trag - gio sì   ne - ro
fall, the   maid - en's heart hath by   thee been per - vert - ed,

drà, sì,   sì,   la   mac - chia d'ol - trag - gio sì ne - ro___ col   tuo
fall, the   maid - en's heart hath by   thee been per - vert - ed,___ We have

Più allegro.

EXERCISE 33.3   Analysis and Dictation of Diatonic and Chromatic Sequences

 Label the sequence type, bracket begin and ending points of the sequence on the incomplete score, then notate the bass line.

A.

B.

(Continued)

(*Continued*)

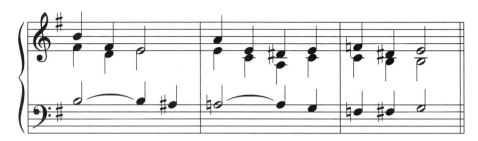

C.

D.

E.   Beethoven, *Scherzo*, Piano Sonata No. 12 in A♭ major, op. 26

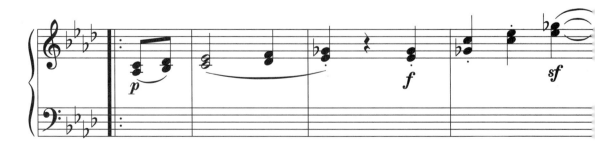

F. Beethoven, *Allegro con brio,* Symphony No. 3 in E♭ major, "Eroica," op. 55

EXERCISE 33.4 Dictation of Sequences

 Identify the sequence type and notate the bass voice.

A.

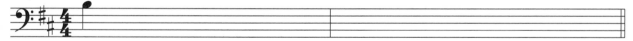

B.

C.

D.

E.

F.   Mendelssohn, *Allegro, un poco agitato,* Symphony No. 3 in A minor, "Scottish," op. 56

G.   Schumann, *Allegro,* Symphony No. 2 in C major, op. 61

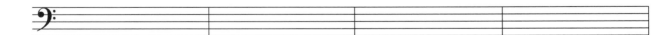

EXERCISE 33.5   Unfigured and Figured Basses

Complete the unfigured bass exercise (A) below in three voices and include 7–6 suspensions. Complete the two figured bass exercises (B and C) in four voices. Label any sequences. Be aware of modulations.

A.

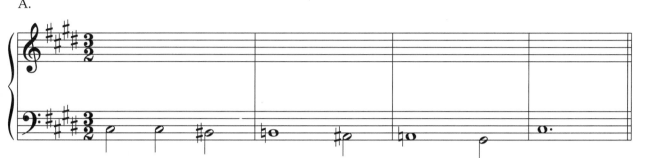

B.

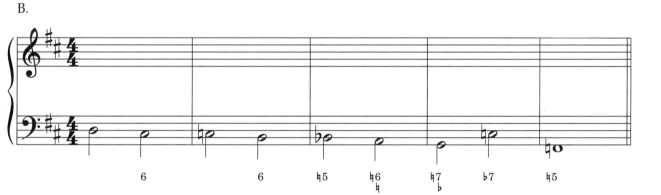

C.

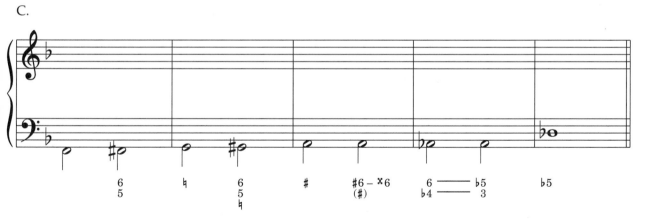

EXERCISE 33.6   Extended Illustrations

Complete the following tasks.

A.   Write a three-voice progression in F♯ minor that begins on tonic, moves through a sequence of descending $^6_3$ chords with 7–6 suspensions and chromatic bass, and leads to a cadential $^6_4$ chord. The dominant will move deceptively to a mixture chord, followed by a cadence in a chromatic third-related key.

B.   Write a three-voice progression in E♭ major that begins with an A2 (D3/A4) sequence using applied V_6 chords that resolve to major triads. This sequence will move from I to III♯. Once you arrive on III♯, treat it as a temporary tonic. Expand and cadence on III♯.

C.   Write a three-voice progression in E♭ major that begins with a chromatic A2 (D3/D4) sequence, this time employing augmented triads that will serve as applied chords to the next chromatic chords. Move from I to III♯ (e.g., I . . . ♭II . . . ♮II . . .). Don't modulate to III♯, but find a convenient way to get back to tonic and cadence there.

D.   Write a four-voice progression in G major that initially moves from I–iv via a chromatic D2 (D4/A3) sequence. Expand this pre-dominant with a voice exchange that includes an augmented sixth chord. Close with a PAC.

EXERCISE 33.7   Analysis of Chromatic Sequences and Contrary-Motion Chromaticism

Label and bracket any sequences in the examples below and analyze any harmonies outside of the sequence.

A.   Brahms, "Salome," op. 69, no. 8

Develop the idea that the chromaticism in this example might have been motivated by the text.

. . . O so bin ich eine Schlang!   . . . I'm a snake!
O ihr Jungfraun im Land,   O you virgins in the country,
Von dem Berg und über See, . . .   From the mountains and across the sea, . . .

B. Schubert, *Allegro*, Violin Sonata in D major, D. 384

C.   Schubert, String Quartet in G major, *Allegro motto moderato*, D. 887

(Continued)

(Continued)

D.   Schubert, Mass in E♭, Sanctus

san - - - ctus,   Do - mi - nus De - us Sa - ba - oth!

EXERCISE 33.8   Dictation

The contrary-motion chromatic progressions prolong either the tonic, the dominant, or the pre-dominant function. Notate outer voices, provide roman numerals, and bracket and label the expanded harmonic function.

A.

B.

C.

EXERCISE 33.9 Figured Bass

Realize the three figured basses below. The first example includes a complete soprano, but the second and third contain incomplete soprano lines. Analyze.

A.

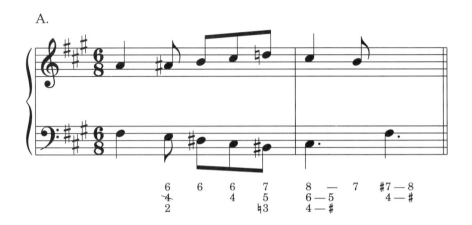

B.

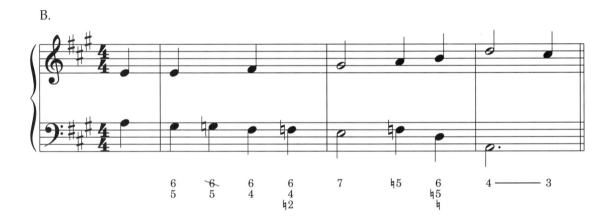

C.

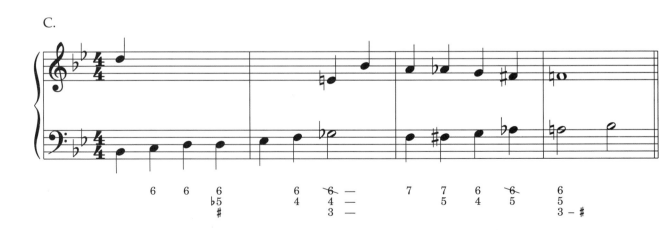

EXERCISE 33.10   Soprano Harmonization

Harmonize in four voices the following soprano melodies; include each of the required elements. Analyze.

A.

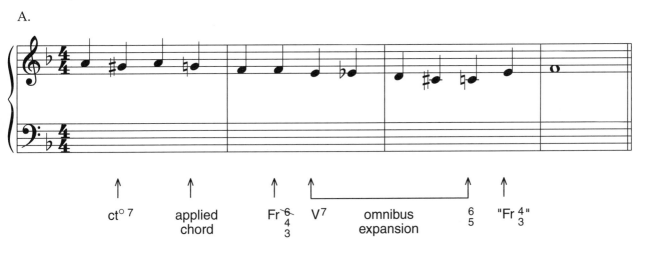

ct° 7   applied   Fr 6   V7   omnibus   6   "Fr 4"
              chord   4   expansion   5   3
                                3

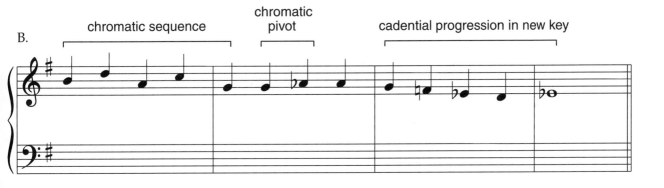

C.

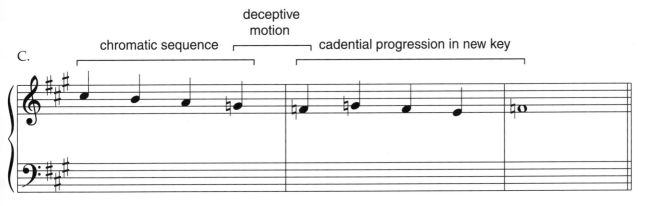

EXERCISE 33.11   Keyboard

Continue the following sequence using chromatic voice exchange (to the key of A♭).

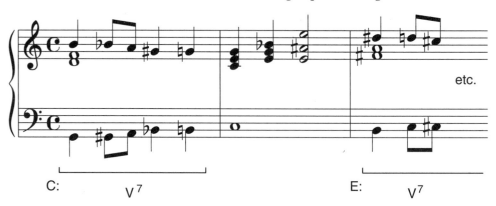

EXERCISE 33.12   Keyboard

Realize the following soprano and figured bass in four voices. Analyze. Be able to sing either outer voice while playing the remaining three.

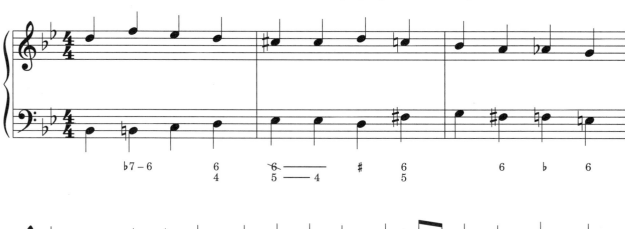

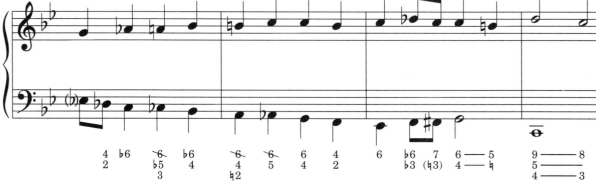

EXERCISE 33.13   Composition

Write two consequents to the given antecedent to create a parallel interrupted period and a contrasting progressive period. Label your periods and analyze the harmonies.

EXERCISE 33.14   Expansion and Variation of Model Progressions

 Study the harmonic models below. Each is followed by a series of expansions and/or variations. Notate outer voices and provide roman numerals. Expect chromatic sequences and modulations.

Model #1:

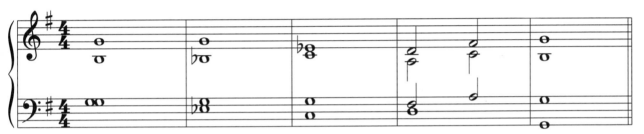

Model #2:

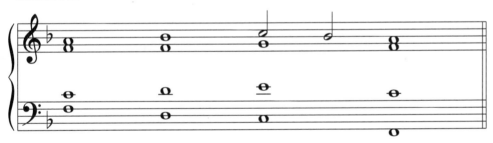

Model #3:

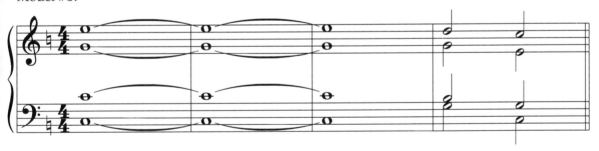

CHAPTER 34

At Tonality's Edge

EXERCISE 34.1   Analysis of Progressions that Divide the Octave Evenly

Use second-level analytical brackets to mark the sequential progression that divides the octave equally into either major or minor thirds, each step of which is tonicized.

A. Brahms, "Immer leiser wird mein Schlummer" ("Ever More Peaceful Grows My Slumber"), op. 105, no. 2

You will encounter several $^6_4$ chords. Some are cadential (e.g., a dominant function) while others are consonant (e.g., a tonic function).

... Wald:
Willst du mich noch einmal sehn,
Komm, o komme bald!

... forest:
If you wish to see me again,
Come, o come soon!

B.   Wolf, "Und steht Ihr früh am Morgen auf" ("And When You Rise Early"),
Italienisches Liederbuch, no. 34

Und steht Ihr früh am Morgen auf vom Bette,	And when you rise early from your bed,
Scheucht Ihr vom Himmel alle Wolken fort,	You banish every cloud from the sky,
Die Sonne lockt Ihr auf die Berge dort,	You lure the sun onto those hills,
Und Engelein erscheinen um die Wette	And little angels compete to come
Und bringen Schuh und Kleider Euch sofort.	And bring you your shoes and clothes.
Dann, wenn Ihr ausgeht in die heil'ge Mette, . . .	Then, when you go out to Mass, . . .

EXERCISE 34.2 Analysis of Non-Sequential Equal Divisions of the Octave

Analyze using second-level analytical brackets to mark the non-sequential progression that divides the octave equally into either major or minor thirds, each step of which is tonicized.

EXERCISE 34.3 Figured Bass

Realize the figured bass below in four voices. Include a roman numeral analysis. Mark all sequences and tonicizations.

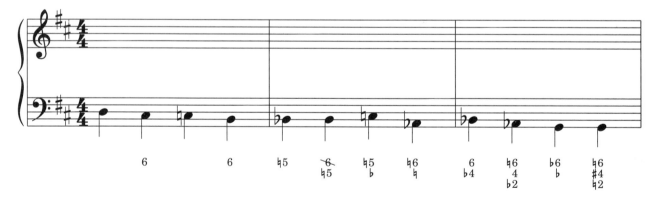

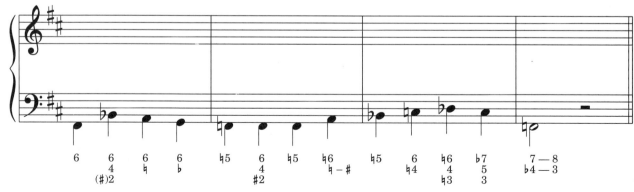

EXERCISE 34.4 Analysis and Dictation: Potpourri of Various Types of Tonicization

The examples below tonicize or modulate to diatonic or chromatic keys. Add missing bass pitches. Analyze. Modulatory techniques include the following:

1. pivot chord (diatonic, mixture chord, or enharmonic [diminished seventh or German sixth]
2. sequence (diatonic or chromatic)
3. sequential progression

A.

B.

C.

D.

EXERCISE 34.5   Unfigured Bass

Consider the harmonic implications of the two-voice counterpoint below. Then, analyze and add the inner voices to create an SATB texture.

EXERCISE 34.6   Figured Bass

Realize the figured bass below in four voices. Analyze and summarize in a sentence or two any large-scale tonal patterns.

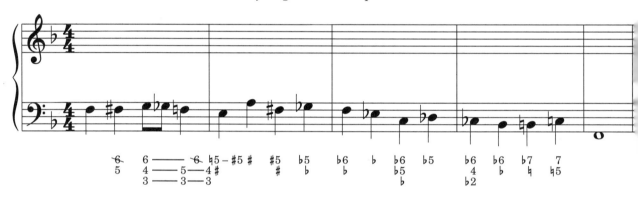

EXERCISE 34.7   Analysis and Dictation

Notate the bass and provide a roman numeral and second-level analysis.

A.   Scriabin, Prelude in A♭ major, op. 11, no. 17

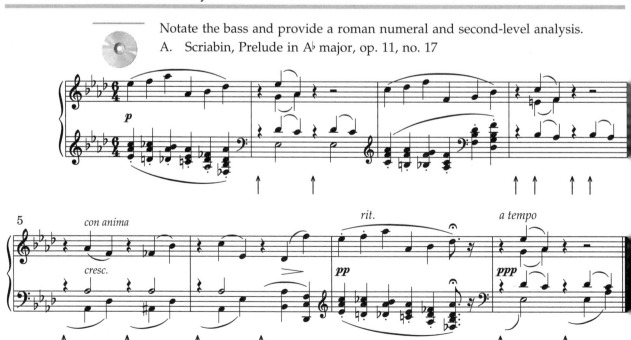

B.   Scriabin, Prelude in C major, op. 35, no. 3

EXERCISE 34.8   Extended Analytical Projects

Analyze the examples that illustrate the compositional techniques covered in Chapters 31 through 34.

A.   Chopin, Mazurka in B major, op. 56, no. 1, BI 153

You are given the opening passages for each of the large sections in Chopin's Mazurka. What is the probable form? Focus on tricky harmonic areas, such as the sequential passage that opens the piece and the transitional and retransitional passages that link larger sections. In a few sentences, discuss what appears to be the large-scale tonal structure of the entire piece.

(Continued)

(Continued)

B.   Below are examples from four of Wagner's operas, *Der fliegende Holländer (The Flying Dutchman)*, *Parsifal*, *Tristan und Isolde*, and *Die Walküre (The Valkyries)*. Analyze each excerpt, then compare and contrast the final three.

1.   "Vorspiel" ("Prelude"), *Der fliegende Holländer (The Flying Dutchman)*

(Continued)

(*Continued*)

2. "Zum letzten Liebesmahle" ("At the Last Meal of Love"), *Parsifal,* act I

(Continued)

(*Continued*)

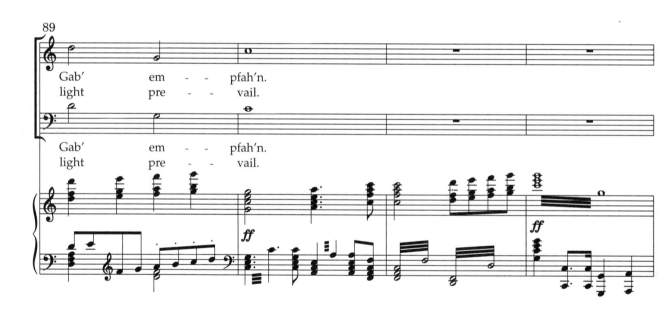

DIE GRALSRITTER

. . . gleich ob zum letzten Male
es heut uns letzen mag,

wer guter Tat sich freut,
ihm wird das Mahl erneut:
der Labung darf er nah'n,
die hehrste Gab' empfah'n.

The Grail Knights

. . . were it to be for the last time,
may it be unsurpassed this day.

If you rejoice in good deeds,
This meal will renew you:
You will be refreshed
With the gift from on high.

3. *Tristan und Isolde,* "Mild und leise" ("Mildly and Gently") (opening of "Liebestod"), act III, scene 3

Mild und leise	Mildly and gently,
wie er lächelt,	how he smiles,
wie das Auge	how his eye
hold er öffnet—	he opens sweetly—
Seht ihr's, Freunde?	Do you see it, friends?
Seht ihr's nicht?	Don't you see it?
Immer lichter	Brighter and brighter
wie er leuchtet,	how he shines,
stern-umstrahlet	star-illuminated
hoch sich hebt?	rises high?

4. "Leb' wohl" ("Live well") ("Woton's Farewell") *Die Walküre (The Valkyries)*, act 3, scene 3

Denn so kehrt	And sadly
der Gott sich dir ab,	The god must depart;
so küsst er die Gottheit von dir!	My kiss removes your godhead!

C.   Berg, "Nacht" ("Night"), *Sieben frühe Lieder*, no. 1

This is the first song in a collection of seven songs that were written just as Berg's compositional voice was beginning to emerge. While written in the shadow of the nineteenth century, these songs also look to the future. We will focus only on the song's opening measures, in which an ambiguous structure gradually gives way to a more traditional harmonic progression, a vivid juxtaposition of old and new styles. Consider these issues in your analysis:

1.   Recall that structure—and with it, clarity—is often postponed until the end of musical units.
2.   Is the key signature unnecessary, or is Berg using it traditionally? If Berg incorporates it traditionally, you may be able to make some harmonic sense out of the opening of the song.
3.   The opening of the song is reminiscent of Scriabin's Prelude, op. 39, no. 2, which was discussed in the text. However, in this song the sonorities owe an even greater debt to the whole-tone scale. Recall from our earlier studies that the whole-tone scale is composed of intervals whose number of half steps is evenly divided by two. For example, a major second (two half steps), major third (four), tritone (six), minor sixth (eight), and minor seventh (ten).
4.   Notice how the song begins with a single pitch, E, to which is added an F♯. Is there some additive process that generates subsequent sonorities?
5.   Study the translation of the text. Is Berg sensitive to its sentiments? If so, how?

Dämmern Wolken über Nacht und Tal,	Over night and valley the clouds grow dark,
Nebel schweben, Wasser rauschen sacht.	Mists are hovering, water rushes by
Nun entschleiert sich's mit einemmal:	Now the covering veil is lifted:
O gib Acht! Gib Acht!	Come look! Look!
Weites . . .	Distant . . .

(Continued)

(Continued)

EXERCISE 34.9   Keyboard: Driving the Omnibus

Play the following progression in keyboard style. Study and play carefully, working the pattern into both your ears and your fingers. Play as written, and then transpose to the key of F major (you'll be starting on C_7, since this omnibus expands the dominant). Then, try leaving the sequence at various points, treating the first chord of any measure as a V_7 (see Example B) or as a Ger 6 (see Example C)

A.

B.

C.

EXERCISE 34.10   Keyboard Brain Twister

Use the following sonorities (or their enharmonic equivalents) in at least two different ways.

A. C♯–E–G–B♭
B. E♭–G–B♭–D♭
C. C–D–F♯–A♭